I DREAM IN BLUE

I DREAM IN BLUE

LIFE, DEATH, AND THE NEW YORK GIANTS

ROGER DIRECTOR

HARPER

An Imprint of HarperCollins*Publishers*
www.harpercollins.com

HarperCollins books may be purchased for educational, business, or sales promotional use. For information, please write: Special Markets Department, HarperCollins Publishers, 10 East 53rd Street, New York, NY 10022.

FIRST EDITION

Designed by Renato Stanisic

FRONTISPIECE: *New York Giants running back Tiki Barber on a touchdown run.* Bob Rosario

Library of Congress Cataloging-in-Publication Data is available upon request.

ISBN: 978-0-06-120913-0
ISBN-10: 0-06-120913-9

07 08 09 10 11 NMSG/RRD 10 9 8 7 6 5 4 3 2 1

*To my two best men—my brother, Jon, and Dave,
my friend and editor for thirty years*

Contents

CHAPTER 1

Amazing Grace 1

CHAPTER 2

And God Created Shockey 15

CHAPTER 3

The Lost City of the Giants 57

CHAPTER 4

Cain, Abel, and Eli 75

CHAPTER 5

1-800-Bite-Me 97

Contents

CHAPTER 6

Once a Giant, Always a Giant 111

CHAPTER 7

Third-and-22 135

CHAPTER 8

Tiki Barber Gets Dressed 159

CHAPTER 9

The Grim Scalper 185

CHAPTER 10

The Final Gun 203

Acknowledgments 225

I DREAM IN BLUE

Alex Webster (left) and Andy Robustelli after the second "sneakers" game in 1956—when my love affair with the team began. HERB SCHARFMAN

Chapter 1

Amazing Grace

The most important decision you're going to make here today is ... if, for whatever reason, something terrible happens ... who do you want to be your daughter's legal guardian?"

The lawyer, Newmark, sits opposite me with a blank lined yellow legal pad and a pen. He looks nothing like what I always imagined the guy putting my affairs in order ought to look like. That lawyer is gray at the temples, somber and distinguished. But Newmark has these little vegetative clumps in odd spots on his pale, scaly scalp; all the groomed gravitas of a vacant lot. Also, he has smallish hands. The capper: He keeps sucking back the saliva he overproduces when he talks.

But I didn't pick Newmark, my wife did. Petite and dark-haired, with a smile the wattage of a ballroom chandelier and a bite like a fer-de-lance, Jan has been trying to get me to sit down with Newmark for months. She's the one who says we need a will.

She wants to make sure our daughter's education is taken care of.

Check. No disagreement there.

Then, understandably, there's making sure that the assets we have will not be taken from her by some humpbacked villain in a black cloak straight out of a silent movie.

No disagreement there. Check.

But a will? Why not hang a sign around my neck saying, Come and Get Me?

So what finally got me here in this conference room looking west over the Pacific Ocean? Maybe it would help to understand if I described how I felt listening to the bagpipes echo on Fifth Avenue that October morning two years ago. How the crowd had gathered outside St. Patrick's Cathedral watching the procession approach.

The crowd was like that for Babe Ruth.

The crowd was like that for Joe DiMaggio.

This crowd was here for a man called the Duke. Wellington Mara. And one could be forgiven for recalling Barbara Tuchman's description of the august funeral procession of Edward VII: "The sun of the old world was setting in a dying blaze of splendor never to be seen again." Gathered in somber pageantry outside and within St. Patrick's were the heads of the varied principalities that made up the world from which the man they honored, Wellington Mara, the owner of the New York Giants football team, had recently departed.

They were the crowned heads from the empire known as the National Football League. They were bent in sorrow and, in some cases, wrinkled and spotted with age. The field marshals and knights-errant who'd ridden to war between the goal lines. The Hall of Fame New York running back Frank Gifford. The unforgettable quarterback Y. A. Tittle. The Giants' former Super Bowl–winning head coach, Bill Parcells, now coaching the Cowboys. Andy Robustelli, the team's Hall of Fame defensive end from its halcyon squads of the '50s. Harry Carson, the Hall of Fame middle linebacker who was instrumental in the Super Bowl XXI victory. Lawrence Taylor, outside linebacker and Hall of Famer, King Kong talked down off the Empire State Building and given Giants' jersey no. 56. And so many more. Five other owners. Four other head coaches. A former mayor of New York. All 2,200 seats were filled.

The New York Giants stepped off seven chartered buses escorted by a New Jersey state patrol car that pulled up in front of the church. And Wellington Mara's immediate football family, the current New York Giants, solemnly stepped off. They filed up the steps and into the cathedral.

"Amazing Grace" was playing. There's a rose window over the Fifth Avenue door and the door was opened and they carried Mr. Mara's casket down the nave. They placed him before the altar, surrounded by bouquets of red roses.

Mara's son, John, spoke. The kingdom's aging prince, Frank Gifford, looking ashen, offered a eulogy. Frank said, "I know we are all suffering from the loss of this great man. But I know, too, we can celebrate one of the incredible lives, and know, too, where he is. He is at the right hand of his longtime head coach in the heavens, his Lord and God."

Afterward, in the silence, flanked by his players, his family and thousands of lifelong fans like me, the people he liked to call his "customers," Wellington Mara's casket was loaded into a hearse, and a horse-drawn carriage led the funeral procession away down Fifth Avenue as the wail of bagpipes rose to the heavens.

That's when I asked myself, as Mara's bier passed from view: What am I leaving behind?

"I presume you two have discussed who your daughter Chloe should live with in the event of your untimely death," Newmark says, prompting us.

"Sure," I say.

We're silent because my wife and I are at loggerheads.

We should have hired RAND to solve this problem. Within minutes of any discussion we had started, we got to calling each other's brothers' and sisters' and mothers' and best friends' homes—places where we regularly enjoy Thanksgiving and Christmas and holiday fun—hotbeds of pederasty and sexual abuse. And the argument was just starting. After one late-night session I hit the wall and told my wife I was dropping out of the discussion. It had gotten too contentious. So I wasn't going to make any more suggestions. I'd just have my one candidate in mind and wait until the time came. I told my wife to go ahead filling up notebooks with lists of qualities and pluses and minuses.

Today, she's brought her own legal pad containing a long list of candidates, in order, with multitudes of well-worked-out reasons pro and con and an accompanying point system. If Chloe goes to my mother-in-law she wouldn't have to change schools. If it's my sister-in-law, she would. If it's my brother or sister she could live on the Upper West Side. One has a nice spare bedroom but there would be no other children in the house, although there's a nice private bathroom. My sister-in-law has kids, but all boys. And poor bathroom door lockage. I got more and more confused evaluating my death in terms of the quality of plumbing facilities it might yield my daughter.

Newmark clicks his pen and slants the notebook, preparing to inscribe the name of the most worthy candidate. "And you?" he asks.

I look at Newmark, and look at my wife, each wondering to whom I'd entrust my most precious belonging. The name comes easily to my lips:

"Tiki Barber."

I am a New York Giants fan. But I make no claim to be a bigger fan than the reader. I don't begrudge those who may be more earnest than me their exalted idiocy. I'm simply saying, don't look within these pages for a catalog of moronic exploits more moronic than the next man's. I do not paint my face. I do not bare my chest. I do not miss meals when my team loses. I could have gotten a free ticket to each game when they advertised for someone willing to sit in the stands and dress up as a Big Blue clown—but I wouldn't. In fact, not doing those things is a mark of education, mature intellect and real purpose.

Rather, think of me simply as someone with shingles or malaria, one of those diseases that rupture the flesh at a fragile age and then disappear for months and years. And then for reasons eternally mysterious to science the disease is retriggered decades later to emerge in the same patient who, it would seem, had long ago lost any connection to that fevered boy beneath the posters in the attic room of the house in which he grew up.

You know that house. A GI loan ranch built for WWII vets coming home from the war.

You know that backyard. The one with the crabgrass and the picnic table and the split-rail fence and the wedge of flower bed in the corner.

You know the street too. It doubled as a football field that ran the length of the curb between two telephone poles marking the goal lines.

The suburban settlers left the cities behind, along with the worlds of their parents. But one thing they never left when they moved was their sports team. That kept them plugged into home soil. And after the steaks had been lifted off the grill, after dessert, after every pantry in the house had been denuded of marshmallows to toast over the last glows of the dying charcoal embers, the older men would sit and talk, using strange words that were as foreign to my ears as their mothers' mother tongues.

"Tuffy Leemans," my uncle Nat would mutter out of the side of his mouth as the dusk came on and the fireflies took wing.

"Ken Strong," my father would reply

I could see the red end of my father's lit cigar as he puffed, removed it from his mouth and said, with a twist, "Here's one for ya: Shipwreck Kelly," exhaling a cloud of smoke. After a moment, I heard the aluminum chairs creaking, shaking with their laughter.

"Benny Friedman."

My father caught me studying him from the screen door, wanting to learn that language.

"A magician with the ball. You didn't know where it was! You couldn't see who had it!"

On a frosty winter afternoon when I was seven my father did something I'd never seen him do before: He set up the radio in a position of grave prominence on our dining room table right in the middle of the house. It was a huge, humped, root-beer-colored Bakelite box that barely fit in my arms and that normally sat in my parents' bedroom. This rearrangement of our internal landscape signaled to me something extraordinary was about to happen. Maybe someone was going to announce something about an atomic bomb.

"Hey, what's this for?" I asked timorously, walking into the house in my hideous puffy gray snowsuit, taking off my red woolen cap with the tassel and the ear flaps, my thighs squeaking—*creet creet creet*—as I headed for the kitchen table and my rendezvous with a glass of milk and two oozing teaspoons of Bosco.

"The Giants game, moron," my older brother Jon said. He was six and a half years my senior and took his job as my tutor in all things—particularly sports—with a purposefulness I might have admired even more if it didn't require him to call me "moron" several times a day.

Whereas Harvard's teaching motto is *Veritas*, my brother's might have been *Puta Rapide*, which roughly translates to: "Think fast." That's what he'd bark at me anytime of the day or night, causing me to look up from a Scrooge McDuck comic at a spiraling football a foot from my forehead. Or a baseball. Or a rubber-tipped arrow. Or a wet bathing suit. Or a slingshot jockstrap. Or a dropping glob of saliva as he sat above, having pinned my shoulders to the ground.

"Think fast, Babe," he'd say. That's his nickname for me. "Babe." He's the only person in the world who calls me that. Been calling me that since I can remember. He'd place my hands around a plastic Wiffle Ball bat and underhand a pitch to me and I'd hack away. I hit lefty. Like Babe Ruth.

"Babe—think fast!"

My brother and father shared something I didn't: the city, during those years after the war. An endless concrete playground where they had begun making the plays that would live forever, the kinds of plays we've all made here and there, even if only once, and maybe not in a Super Bowl or a college game or a high school game, the kind Irwin Shaw described in his short story, "The Eighty-Yard Run." Maybe you made the play at the schoolyard in a pickup game, or a backyard somewhere, or the street outside your house.

My arrival forced a change of venue and, who could blame my father and brother, I suppose, for being unhappy about having the game interrupted? The sawed-off stickball bats taken from their hands and broken in two over suburban America's knee. The leather shoulder pads left somewhere in a box in the building basement and lost, or now, perhaps, having survived the incinerator, been unpacked in an unfinished attic within the ranch house, relaced and actually trotted out for a game, only to seem suddenly useless, cheap, lackluster, embarrassing in the bright sunshine gleaming off the new plastic ones worn by the kids on the green suburban gridiron.

My father and brother had their history. And they had their team: the New York football Giants.

The 1956 NFL championship game from Yankee Stadium was the first one I heard, the broadcast blasting from the Bakelite box on the mahogany dining room table. It was as delightful as a childhood dream could be, what with my father and older brother and I crowded around, straining to hear the ins and outs of every play while my mother moved about the kitchen preparing dinner. Everything the Giants did worked. Everything the Chicago Bears tried didn't. The Giants scored on the second play of the game and, seemingly, every time they touched the ball. They led at halftime, 34–7.

"Who's Frank Gifford?" I asked, after a Giants player by that name caught a long pass against someone named J. C. Caroline, who fell down trying to cover him.

"He's a triple threat, that's what he is," my brother said.

"A triple threat is someone who can run and pass and kick," my father explained.

"Gifford was named All-Pro on defense and on offense two straight years," my brother added impatiently.

"If he's so good, then why do they give the ball to Mel Triplett?" I asked.

"Moron," my brother said, and he leaped out of his chair and demonstrated how number 33 bucked into the line like a charging rhino and threw off tacklers.

My father and brother were communing in some private ecstasy. I quickly copied their jubilation, and they let me in.

"That Robustelli is some player, man alive," my father said.

My brother showed me a picture of the defensive end Andy Robustelli, which he'd clipped from a newspaper the week before. I liked him right away. Liked his friendly name, which didn't sound so scary—Andy. He had big hands. Rough, like my father's. He had raccoon eyes with sloping brows and he seemed ready to get you in a mighty bear hug that looked like it might stop you but wouldn't necessarily hurt all that much, kind of like the way my brother wrapped me up when he would wrestle me down in the hallway.

"The Giants are smart. They're wearing sneakers," my father said.

"Why aren't the Bears wearing sneakers?" I asked. "I wear sneakers when I play football."

"Moron," my brother said. "Normally, they wear cleats. You see how frozen it is outside? Like ice. The Bears' cleats can't get a grip. They're slipping all over the place. But the Giants' sneakers give them traction."

I imagined the Chicagoans, flailing and sliding and slipping and missing as Frank Gifford and Mel Triplett and Kyle Rote squirted and darted by toward the end zone. And on defense, the proud, burly owners of a host of rough-sounding, rugged-syllabled names—Katcavage, Huff, Robustelli, Modzelewski—seemed to rise up out of the radio box like a giant blue wave drowning any Bear who was unfortunate enough to be holding the pigskin.

How could a team show up wearing the wrong shoes? That was like showing up for gym without your sneakers and trying to play in your Thom McAns. Nothing in my life had dumbfounded me like this: a professional sports team showing up for the big game and not bringing the right footwear!

"And this isn't the first time they wore sneakers against the Bears, you know," my father said between puffs on his cigar, a Webster Fancy Tail that I had watched him purchase with intense fascination on the way home from his office the previous Saturday. He had taken me to work with him and we had stopped off at Nat Sherman's, where he inspected and rolled and squeezed and sniffed the merchandise before deciding on his buy and thrusting it into a manila envelope.

"There was actually a game called 'the Sneakers Game,'" he continued. "That was back in, uh . . . let's see . . . it must have been '34 or '35 . . . Those were tough times, I tell you . . . the whole country was out of work. There were no jobs. People had nothing to eat! Man alive. Things were bad. Bad, I tell you. You were lucky if you made a nickel a day. A nickel! So it must have been '34. . . . Anyway, the Bears were good that year. They'd won I don't know how many straight games. And they were ahead at halftime. But it was freezing outside. The field was icy. And the Giants came out in the second half and what do you know? They were wearing sneakers! Sneakers! I mean, that was unheard of. Sneakers! But they could plant their feet and the Bears couldn't, and Ken Strong scored two touchdowns and the Giants won. That game was called 'the Sneakers Game.' "

As the Giants romped to a blissfully easy 47–7 victory, I decided in my warm suburban den that New York's football team was the shrewdest team in the world. Its players, its coaches, its equipment managers—everyone down to its hot dog vendors and ticket takers—were the best, and the city they all represented was far and away the cleverest and most resourceful. I decided, too, that Giants fans, by implication, were also the smartest, the toughest, the best. Unbeatable. How stupid must anyone who lived in Chicago be to allow the same dumb mistake to happen twice, not bringing along a box of sneakers for their team in case the field was just as frozen as it had been back then in the Great Depression, when my dad had to work so hard. It was common sense.

"You stupid oafs!" I could hear my father telling the Bears and their longtime leader, George Halas.

"They're morons," my brother said, and I felt a thrill to hear that word land on someone else for a change. Only a momentarily thrill, however, like the one Larry got watching Moe hit Curly.

The joy that radiated between my father and older brother enfolded me too that Sunday afternoon. My childhood became unbeatable. My city was unbeatable. My team was unbeatable. Yankee Stadium was unbeatable. The Giants were unbeatable. I was seven years old, and my brother and my father and I were unbeatable, too.

The late Wellington Mara on the sidelines at training camp in 1994. "I know . . . he is at the right hand of his longtime head coach in the heavens, his Lord and God," Frank Gifford said at his funeral. GABE PALACIO

Chapter 2

And God Created Shockey

There are almost no circumstances under which it is possible to envision oneself spending any time in a place as dreary and dismal as Albany, New York, but this is where the Giants summer.

And so shall I. Ever leery of ripping apart my chest walls with my own bare hands, wedging my fingernails into the space between my ribs and tearing them apart as you would crack open a crab, and presenting my fully exposed, beating heart to the team I fear will rip it out.

It's going to sound ridiculous, but I was sent here by Newmark. Not literally, but as an outgrowth of that meeting. He's helped to set it in motion: the Year of the Will. Newmark had me sign something that said I wasn't a kid anymore. Well, let's take one last look to see who that kid was before I lock him away in a safe-deposit box.

And here's a good starting place for the accounting process. Going to Albany with the Giants is not the most unlikely thing for me to be doing, actually. Long ago, before becoming a television producer, I was a sportswriter, an editor at the now-defunct *Sport* magazine. I plan to follow the Giants around for the upcoming season. I have left my home in Santa Monica and flown across the country to join Big Blue in training camp fifty years after the Giants beat the Bears in that championship game I had listened to on the big brown Bakelite radio in the dining room alongside my brother and father.

Training camp is hard on the Giants, especially because their coach, Tom Coughlin, acts as if he carries a copy of Captain Bligh's how-to book in his back pocket. But at least the players are well fed. Overseen by experts who attend to every bruise and strain, who strap them together, scope and clean out their frayed joints, knead sore muscles, even talk out tenderized psyches. They have agents to coddle them; families, in most cases, to support them; and trainers and medical staff to keep them playing. They have film to help them correct their mistakes.

What about me?

I have nothing. The only people who have any vested interest in my well-being are three thousand miles away. And the only words of support I've gotten about coming to Giants training camp and seeing what will happen this season have been "Why the fuck would you want to do that?"

My wife thinks I'm sick. Not just in the head, but really sick. For a long time she couldn't put her finger on it, but she insisted something was wrong with me every time she told me we needed a will and I resisted. I was in perfectly good health. Vital. Living life on two coasts. I eat well. I sleep well. I shit well. I piss well. I fuck well enough. I play basketball once a week. I can open any jar. Change any lightbulb.

"Do I look like I'm about to die?" I asked my wife whenever she brought up the subject.

And that's what I said to my wife for the umpteenth time a few months ago, and here's what happened: She went into the computer room and returned fifteen minutes later waving a printout.

"I knew it—you have RLS," she said. It still pisses me off, that note of triumph in her voice.

"What is RLS?" I asked.

"Restless leg syndrome."

"I'm trying to watch some football highlights, if you don't mind," I said.

"Every seventeen seconds in your sleep your legs spasm," she said. "It's like clockwork. Every seventeen seconds. You flail your legs and sometimes even your arms. I can't sleep. Your twitching is driving me crazy."

She had it all right there on the printout. Restless Leg Syndrome. Uncontrollable seizures in the middle of the night.

"I never heard of anything called RLS," I told her as she sat down next to me on the sofa in our den.

"What's going on?" she asked. "What was *that*?" She looked at me with alarm.

"The Giants just gave up a touchdown, obviously," I said, trying not to sound sulfurously patronizing.

"I don't mean that, I mean *that*," she said, banging her right leg hard against my left.

"That?"

"Yeah, that's what you do at night in bed. That's what I'm

talking about. Those movements. Now you're doing it while you're awake, too?" she asked.

I realized, although I couldn't admit it to her, that I was straining my body like that in the same way that, on the TV screen, one of the Giants, Osi Umenyiora, was straining to overtake and tackle an opposing running back.

I caught myself twitching the same way on the next play. I discovered I was doing this on every play—clenching with isometric empathy.

"What is that?" my wife kept saying, looking like she'd seen a snake, shrinking back in alarm.

"It's nothing," I said.

But I started thinking: Maybe these empathic spasms had taken on a life of their own. Maybe I was playing with the Giants in my sleep. In my dreams.

Camp is at the state university. The campus was midwifed by then–Governor Nelson Rockefeller and designed by Edward Durell Stone in the International style in vogue in the middle of the last century. Stone did well by the family with his early work on Rockefeller Center, but you can't help feeling that Rocky must have been too busy putting the full Nelson on blond nymphette stenographers in his midtown Manhattan townhouse to have thought better about what would happen if he let Stone near a college campus. Stone came up with a plan for the new University of the Androids. Soulless, overly grandiose twenty-three-story dorms spike into the sky anchoring four quads, leaving the rest of the campus an amorphous sea of continuous low roofs and concrete loggias.

My training camp headquarters are even less people-friendly. And they are not the legacy of a world-famous architect. Far from it. My training camp headquarters are a few miles away right off Interstate 90 at the Clarion Hotel, whose dark, mute, soiled confines—including the long, hellish, fluorescent-lit hallway to the cheap cinder-block rear annex, the tiny alcove with the mini washer-dryer, the petri dish they called a pool, the plastic, Formica, sticky-boothed coffeeshop—would have been a good location for a horror movie. The slow, whining ascent rate of the elevator seemed a comment on the fact that no one in this hotel, or, for that matter, in Albany, had anything important to do or anywhere to be. The doors opened with a pained groan, revealing, floor by floor, the same stacked-up room service trays that remained uncollected for days.

Truly, the slower the elevator, the better. I put the time to good use, staring at my reflection in the mirror, proudly wearing my Giants credential admitting me to the camp down the road. It has a picture of a football helmet on it. I'm not gonna say I wore it to sleep. But I put it on as soon as I got up.

If I'm in the Clarion, shuffling along the breakfast buffet line, sleepily wielding that huge plastic scoop to deposit into my paper cereal bowl what can best be described as kibble, I'm wearing my Giants credential. In the tiny cubicle where they have the washer and dryer, I'm wearing my Giants credential. I wear my Giants credential everywhere I go in Albany, including the Gateway Diner right down Central Avenue, and I always get a good seat, especially when no one else is there. Once, on a gusty day, the wind blew so hard it twirled my credential around like a weathervane, so that the string holding it around my neck began to tighten like a noose and I was almost strangled to death by my own credential.

At 8:40 A.M. on July 31, the 2006 Giants take the field and form half a dozen sideline-to-sideline ranks spanning one of the three practice fields. This is a stirring sight, a tap on the shoulder reminding the autumn equinox not to tarry.

Behold the Giants!

Behold them in their relaxed pride as they stretch and flex and the assistant coaches count cadences.

"Stay behind the red line, please."

At camp the journalists are kept in a little pen. It's right off the field, but they paint a tiny red rectangle on the grass and if you step out of it a sixteen-year-old girl will come up and will unkindly instruct you to get back. More than a few times, when I stretch a little too far forward to watch Chad Morton return punts or Brandon Jacobs gallop downfield, I'm reminded that few things smart like the voice of a pissy teenaged girl. Even herded in my little red pen, I'm still close, though. I can feel the wind swirling in Tiki Barber's wake when he bulls up the sideline.

The most noticeable man on the field isn't here. The Duke. Wellington Mara. The owner, son of the founder, was on that sideline every year for over eighty years, beginning in 1925. Since before they put up the first Christmas tree in Rockefeller Center. Since he was merely Big Tim's little kid. Everybody at the camp—the line and backfield coaches running drills, the players, the trainers (including peppery John Johnson, now well into his eighties, who has been with the team since the late '40s and who helped Frank Gifford off the field in 1960 after the hit from Bednarik and whose fingers are crooked from a lifetime of tearing tape and who *still* tapes Michael Strahan's ankles every day, at Strahan's insistence)—sees Wellington Mara sitting there in his porkpie hat on his portable chair in sun and rain. Even though he died nine months ago. Open your eyes or close them, it doesn't matter. Wellington Mara is burned into the retina.

"The last game Mr. Mara saw was against the Denver Broncos," Tiki Barber, the peerless Big Blue running back, had told me at a lunch that spring. *"As a Giants fan, you know ten years ago there was no way in hell we would win that game, you know what I mean? There's no way. But for some reason we've developed the resiliency to come back and fight and we won that Denver game and it was beautiful.*

"And that started off what was an astounding week for me. Because we won that game Coach Coughlin gave us Monday off. Halfway through that Monday, Ronnie Barnes, who is our head trainer, called me and said, 'The Maras would like you to come up and see Wellington.' You know, they think he's in his last hours or couple of days and so me and Jeremy Shockey went up.

"Jeremy got there before I did. I got lost getting to his house. And so Jeremy was leaving when I got there. And so I had an opportunity really to spend alone time with Mr. Mara, you know . . . thank him . . . say a prayer with him, and tell him how much I appreciated all that he gave to me, the opportunities he gave to me.

"I don't know if he heard me, but I think he did. And subse-

quently I was the last player to see him alive. Which at the time I didn't really think about. But as the week went on I did.

"We had his funeral at St. Patrick's. It was a perfect day for a funeral. It was overcast but it was crisp. You know, very high clouds, but it was crisp. For whatever reason—circumstance, faith—I ended up being the guy leading our team into St. Patrick's Cathedral. It was a beautiful, phenomenal service. John gave the most moving tribute to his father and he encapsulated him perfectly.

"And when the funeral was over we went outside. And then, you know, it was a surreal scene. The other side of the street on Fifth Avenue was packed with people. You know, just paying their respects.

"So, being that Tom Coughlin was our coach, we had to go back and practice afterward. It was absolutely weird. But we get to the stadium and literally as soon as we sit down to start stretching, there was this break in the clouds. It looked fake, because it was just a beam of light right on our practice . . . right on our practice field, and it didn't last long . . . maybe five minutes . . . but Tom was walking by me and I said, 'Tom, that's Mr. Mara looking down on us.' And he said, 'You know, I think you're right.'

"So then we go to play the game on Sunday against Washington, and they're one of our biggest foes. And the first play of the game I had a fifty-seven-yard run. And then I had another fifty-something-yard run. I mean, I was in a zone, you know? It didn't matter what play we called. I knew it was going to work.

"And Timmy McDonnell, who is Mr. Mara's grandson, he came over and he was fussing on me. He said, 'Dude, are you going to keep getting caught or are you going to score a touchdown?'

"I'm like, 'Timmy, I promise you I'll score you a touchdown before my day is done.'

"And so probably three minutes left in the third quarter, we're

driving again and again I'm, you know, in the zone and we get down to the four-yard line or whatever and I'm three yards away from breaking my career best. And we call a draw. I make a guy miss, jump over a guy, get to the end zone.

"Then I get up and do what I always do, I blow a kiss. I drop the ball and as soon as I blew the kiss, I remember and I went back and grabbed the ball. And I ran right over to the sidelines and gave it to Timmy and I said, 'Timmy this is for you and your grandfather. We love you, man.'

"And then I took myself out of the game. And a lot of people were like, why did he come out? You know, he was only six yards away from the Giants' career rushing record in a game. But I was done. You know. That was the perfect way for me to end that game. I had made Mr. Mara's grandson a promise. And I kept it.

"It was what will be the most memorable day of my career. I ended with a touchdown and keeping a promise. And then I sat down in the fourth quarter. I mean, I could have rushed—I guarantee I could have rushed for three hundred yards. I had no doubt in my mind. But it was enough, because it wasn't about me, it was about what I could do for the Mara team, for the Mara family. And then, literally, I got home and broke down crying."

In his father's place as team president, son John, fifty-two, slender and taller than his dad, could be mistaken for any of the dozens of spectators who've paid the bucks to sit on the adjacent hillside or cluster along the temporary fencing in Bermuda shorts and T-shirts. Of clerkish affect, with no sign of his pop Wellington's bulldog jaw, you could take John Mara for an easy mark. Like he'd bite on a three-card monte game. He is desperately in need of sunblock and headed for a good, old-fashioned, fair-skinned Irish sunburn.

John is as self-effacing as his father was. So is his younger brother Chris, who is the kind of guy you could stare at across an airport waiting room for ten minutes before you realized, Oh, hey, that's Chris. No, Tim Mara's grandsons are not high rollers. This makes it easier to fancy yourself owning such a football team and standing here on the sidelines, squinting into the summer sun and watching several hundred million dollars in muscles that you lease go through their drills.

To the extent that training camp is a get-ready-for-the-real-thing drill, it's something like preproduction. Everyone learning his lines, so to speak. Everyone getting ready everything that will be required. And the beginning of training camp is like the first day of shooting on the set. You don't want your first shot to be too difficult. You want to get the crew working in sync, in rhythm, feeling good. You want it to go well, get everyone off on the right foot, make everyone look good, and successfully finish the first day's work.

A few minutes into practice on this bright Monday morning, Eli Manning takes the snap and drops back to pass. All eleven starters from last year's effective offense are in formation. Tight end Jeremy Shockey. Right tackle Kareem McKenzie. Right guard Chris Snee. Center Shaun O'Hara. Left guard Dave Diehl. Left tackle Luke Pettigout. Wide receiver Amani Toomer. Wide receiver Plaxico Burress. Quarterback Manning. Fullback Jim Finn. And Tiki Barber, the greatest running back in the history of the franchise.

This is Manning's first pass of the season. No one can know

in what stadium or against which team many months from now his last pass will be thrown. We don't know, of course, which of the two fates destined for every pass—complete or incomplete—awaits it. But if your last pass of the season, where and whenever it comes, falls incomplete, it's more than a little likely your season's not ending on a high note.

Therefore, you want the first pass of the season to be good—as good as it can be. At the very least, you want it completed.

So Manning, the twenty-five-year-old son of the great Archie Manning and the younger brother of Peyton Manning—who people are beginning to call the greatest quarterback of all time—lets fly the first pass of the third season of his professional career. This is the season he is expected to display fully mature, ripened star skills. This season will finally reveal what the upside of Peyton's little brother can be. This season will also determine the legacy of retiring general manager Ernie Accorsi, who moved heaven, earth and the future of the franchise to draft Manning and who has announced this will be his last year. And it will likely determine the future of straitlaced coach Tom Coughlin, beginning his third year at the helm with both Super Bowl expectations and rumors of player dissatisfaction in the air. With everyone's future riding on this moment, Manning fades back to pass.

Manning's pass seems to leave a vapor trail against the blue sky as it arches for sixty yards, streaking high and fast and deep. And it comes down perfectly into the hands of the rubbery, 6-5 Burress, who has faked out and left far behind the Giants' new cornerback, Sam Madison, who was acquired in the off-season from Miami.

Onlookers cheer. The pass pops open a champagne cork in your head.

There may be thirty-one other such perfectly thrown and caught passes on thirty-one other first snaps as NFL camps open around the country; it may be this is merely a good show, a well-produced first take. But that doesn't belittle the flutter you feel in your stomach watching such a hookup.

The Giants commence practicing for the next five months of their lives, breaking into squads. Defensive backs, receivers, defensive linemen, offensive linemen.

"Smash step . . . smash step . . . smash step!" the new DB coach, Peter Giunta, hollers at his squad of defensive backs as they try to push off-stride receivers releasing from the line of scrimmage.

Michael Strahan, the All-Pro defensive end, lines up to swat and slalom his way through a forest of heavy practice dummies with "arms" sticking out from them so that it looks like he's charging through a field of saguaro cacti.

" 'Ey, I'd like to see you try this just once," Strahan says, sweat pouring off him, leaning into his taunt while bantering with one of his coaches before taking the first run through the drill. The rest of the defensive linemen stand, hands on hips, behind him: the sun-blotting figures of Osi Umenyiora, Fred Robbins, William Joseph. The tapered physique of Justin Tuck, in his second year out of Notre Dame, who cannot know that his season, for which he so assiduously sweats, will last just three games. Nor can Strahan know his will last just half the year. Nor can obelisk-slim Mathias Kiwanuka, the Giants' top pick out of Boston College, know that upon his shoulders—which have never worn pads in a professional game—the team's fortunes will largely ride. (Asked if he has practiced a signature "sack dance" to utilize over the body of a tackled opposing quarterback, he answers with an unaffected giggle in the summer shade during a break: "No, I think I have to try it out on my teammates first before I use it in a game.")

Kiwanuka is the latest addition to retiring Ernie Accorsi's quarterback-devouring raptors, whose goal is to arrive at the spot from which the opposing quarterback intends to hurl a pass in little more than three seconds. The linemen douse themselves in deluges of water, squirting through hoses attached to coolers constantly wheeled around after them.

"Stay behind the red line, please."

Tom Coughlin's football camp is like living in a barracks in Baghdad's Green Zone. Credentials. Checkpoints. Friends and family having to wait outside and downstairs. Off-limits to reporters. The only thing missing is guard dogs. The atmosphere used to be looser. Coughlin's predecessor, Jim Fassel, who coached the team from 1997 to 2003, enjoyed himself. Liked and could tell jokes. Schmoozed with the writers. Would bullshit on the phone. Seemed like the kind of guy who would appreciate a lap dance. As opposed to Tom Coughlin, who probably wouldn't admit to having a lap. Coughlin looks like a guy in whose office you'd go over the map for the Allied attack on Düsseldorf. Once the battle starts he winds up running around and waving his arms wildly in the air. Ultimately, he appears so easily provoked he seems tormented.

Each summer, one particularly devoted Giants fan shows up at camp (a few hundred are there to watch each day). Fassel took a liking to this fan and when the team broke camp Fassel would invite the fan onto the center of the field, where he'd raise the Giants flag high amid the players and lead the team in cheers for the upcoming season.

But Coughlin found no place in his regulations for a guy with a painted face waving a Giants banner around on his practice field, so he had the guy relegated with everyone else behind the fencing.

"Stay behind the red line, please!"

Coughlin seems to believe that the more schedules and rules there are, the closer together the team will be. "No team can be a winner if its players aren't close," he repeatedly says, and then he staples them together with rules and regulations. What you come to realize is that the one ingredient missing from this perfect picture of summer and football and training camp is fun.

"Have fun," I implore the Giants' new linebacker, LeVar Arrington, in the locker room one day, and he just looks at me like the hairs in my nostrils have come to life and begun doing the Charleston and fixes me with a Freon-cold stare.

"Have fun!?" he declaims with a sour snort, looking around as if he were in the exercise yard at Alcatraz.

You get the feeling sometimes that Coughlin would send the stewards looking for the missing frozen strawberries, à la another great leader named Queeg. He's always running and flapping around the sidelines, the opposite of other coaches, like, for example, the Jets' new young coach, Eric Mangini, who are symbols of planted imperturbability. One might think a coach who stresses conformity over individuality would be a model of behavior. I wasn't surprised to hear Accorsi allude to what a nervous Nellie Coughlin was and what a pain in the ass it was to have a coach like that. Jumping around like Daffy Duck invokes the burlesque—cream pies in the face, banana peels to slip on, chaos, the laughable. As opposed to the volumes of motivational therapy a mere stare from Mangini imparts. Coughlin transmits the message, "We need help or we'll fall apart," as opposed to, "We'll get the job done."

Rules do not necessarily improve morale. Not a few pro athletes enjoy the pay grade and entourage of a movie or TV star. Consideration and respect is the way to get great work out of talent, not rules for rules' sake. Rules may eat away at morale even though, as with all rules, they have been imposed "for your own good."

Take the cleat rule. Coughlin has a rule that the players remain in their football cleats while traveling to meetings. If this was designed to prevent the players from walking around in high heels, it might be reasonable. But the players get their feet twisted, gouged, stepped on, and fractured for hours at a time. When they're not on the field they'd love to kick off their shoes and give their feet a rest.

At lunch, the players don't walk up from their dorm, which is only a quarter mile from the cafeteria where everyone eats—they hop into their Escalades. (They don't all drive Escalades, obviously, but the only ride I saw that you wouldn't find in the valet line at the country club was owned by Michael Jennings, a superfast receiver who barely made the team and drives pure, raked-up street muscle.) It saves time, if not gas. Plus, there is no better way of restoring the sense of individuality and control over one's pace and destination, if only for an hour at lunch, before getting back on Coach Coughlin's schedule—where, famously, as if taken out of *Alice in Wonderland*, if you aren't five minutes early to a meeting you're fined for being late.

The Escalades are air-conditioned, too. And in addition to allowing them to get behind the wheel of their Escalade and boom the music, the brief car ride spares their feet. Going into and out of lunch, there's the steady *clack-clack* of plastic flip-flops snapping on relieved and unencumbered toes as they herd toward the food.

Otherwise they're in cleats. The cleat rule proves costly very quickly because cleats are, well, for football fields and not for Edward Durell Stone's polished dormitory floors. The first week of camp, promising backup ball carrier Derrick Ward, following the rules and wearing his cleats on the slippery dorm stairs, breaks his foot. He misses half the season, not to return to active duty until the fateful Bears game in Week 9. Until then he has little to do but rehab and imagine shoving his cleat a mile up Coughlin's ass.

The Giants practice like maniacs. Manning, then his backups—Tim Hasselbeck, Jared Lorenzen, and veteran Rob Johnson, a favorite of Coughlin's who doesn't make the final cut—take five snaps, then step aside. The team's Russell Crowe look-alike, tight end Jeremy Shockey, comes off the line like a Funny Car in a drag race. When the Giants practice a running play, Tiki Barber dodges through the line at full speed. Defenders react, slapping at Tiki instead of tackling him. Tiki doesn't stop once he's passed the line. He runs for 60, 70 yards. Way downfield. Beyond everybody.

"Stay behind the red line, please."

Barber has the advantage of most "small" runners. He is hard for tacklers to find. Maybe being a twin helps in some peculiar way—the results of a life spent in the investigation of hiding in plain sight. Maybe being a twin helps you not be tackled. You are always someplace else.

Barber's ascension began in the late 1990s, after the Giants lost faith in Tyrone Wheatley. In the league's first draft, in 1936, the Giants picked George Washington's Tuffy Leemans, and he wound up in the Hall of Fame. In general, the team's record for drafting running backs when it needed them is pretty good. Not just Frank Gifford, taken in the first round in '52, but others who were durable, if not spectacular, and could move the chains: Allie Sherman's fave Joe Morrison, third round out of Cincinnati in '59; Tucker Frederickson, round 1 out of Auburn in '65; Joe Morris, a second-rounder from Syracuse in '82; Rodney Hampton, a top pick in '90 from Georgia.

Then there have been the great failures, names inscribed on the Ferdinand de Lesseps Trophy (named after the Frenchman who fucked up the first Panama Canal). Wheatley, a No. 1 pick from Michigan in 1995, stood atop the list, rushing for less than 1,300 yards in four years. (Nothing should give Wheatley any greater satisfaction than the Giants' drafting Ron Dayne, the 2000 Heisman Trophy winner, whose epic—and sole—achievement as a Giant was, after four years, to erase Wheatley's name from the record book as the highest-picked flop ever to carry a ball for the team.) In the second round of the 1997 draft, Tiki Barber became a New York Giant.

Barber's running style is not flashy. Players have created an entire postgraduate curriculum in dramatic arts, inventing ways to celebrate a touchdown and, in the end, they uniformly look silly. They throw the ball onto the ground with all their might. They spin it to the ground so that it twirls on its end like a top. Or they heave it into the stands. Or hurl it against the stadium walls in explosive catharsis. Or dunk it over the crossbar. Or some variation on the theme of furiously expelling from their person the burden of the ball they have been laboring to carry. At the other extreme, some care for the ball. They perform CPR on the ball. Or they rock the ball like a baby. Not to mention all the bizarre jigs and dances.

Tiki blows kisses.

He's blowing them to his family at home. Love and regard in place of combativeness and disdain. How brilliant!

He would never be called "Crazy Legs" or "Iron Head." Barber does not skate, does not lope. He is not a water bug, not a will-o'-the-wisp and certainly not a mule or a tank. You could compare him to another smallish back, Tony Dorsett, but then again, Tiki doesn't explode squared up through the hole like Dorsett. The problem he poses to a defense as he carries the ball is more like this: Three Mercedes sedans have just burst out of a dance club driveway, each speeding separate ways, and the defense, like the paparazzi, has to figure out which one is carrying Lindsay Lohan.

Not easy to pinpoint.

And not easy to knock off his feet. He's tough. A great cutback runner. Meaning Tiki's thinking ahead of you. Not just on a football field, either. His running has the liquid quality of thought.

For the last few years he has been, in his phrase, "playing the game on a different level," the way one of his favorite players, Marshall Faulk, could do. If you ask Tiki what his best physical asset is he might say it's his "flexible ankles." They help him cut. And, more important, "give" with the hits, so that Tiki has remained remarkably injury-free. He puts the maximum pressure on the defense on every play, running expertly behind his blockers, spacing out the defenders until some spot along the point of attack sags or "creases," to use Tiki's verb. Then, with the abrupt power of a jumping frog (he was a state long jump champ in high school), he cuts ambitiously up the field.

"You always look for the crease," he says. "But the thing is, you've got to—you've kind of got to be going at it, at least in the general vicinity and not knowing where it's going to be . . . but you can't be hesitant. You know, a lot of good backs can't find the crease. And that's why they average three yards a carry.

"It's anticipation; it's knowing where it's supposed to be. Like when you watch the Denver Broncos, you know, they got in trouble a couple of years ago because all they do . . . every single lineman makes a crease, do you know what I mean? Every single one of them. They go up and then they cut you. Sometimes illegally. But they're all making creases, and that's why every running back in that system rushes for 1,500 yards, because there are creases.

"So you really have your choice and you can take the biggest crease, you know? You just have to make one or two guys miss and you have a lot of big runs."

"*Stay behind the red line, please!*"

At 11:40 an air horn blasts and they break for lunch. They

hit the showers. Maybe study or pick up DVDs that have been broken down for them to play and replay, dissecting every lean, every block, every placement of their every step. Plaxico Burress stays behind. He positions himself death-wish close to a machine that automatically shoots footballs at him at 80 miles an hour. Snap snap snap. The footballs explode at him and are swallowed up into Burress's soft hands.

Coughlin dutifully tramps across the grass for a few minutes to field questions from the press. Coughlin is about as garrulous as former attorney general John Ashcroft. He'll say what he has to say in his hoarse voice and say it again if you make him, but that's all you're going to get. Coughlin mounts a step stool so he stands a foot and a half above the cone of media, who supplicatingly focus their tape and video recorders and pads and pencils at him so as not to miss a syllable of whatever unmemorable comments he has to say.

That gleaming rainbow pass from Eli to Burress has started camp the right way. The perfect way. And then there is Tiki. The way he dips off right tackle, led by those jumbos in pads and shorts. The defense hustles to cut him off. You don't hear the smack of pads—this is not hitting. But without that, and without the usual sound of fans cheering, you hear something even more thrilling: the stampeding feet. You feel the ground thrum as they chase. The hairs on your neck stand. Thunder rumbles through your shoes. Your own flight-and-run instinct is activated. You hear the click of grinding teeth, the wild rasp of furiously bellowing lungs pumping air through dilating nostrils. Tons of huge guys pounding. All aimed at Tiki Barber.

But he beats them to the corner. He rushes by you. Inches from you . . .

"I saw Tiki Barber today. Had lunch with him. Invited me to join him. Sat right next to him. Just him and me."

I'm back at my camp, the diamond in the necklace of Albany's elite hostelry, where there are two sofas in the lobby. I like to relax there after a long day and flaunt Coach Coughlin's "cleat rule." Two guys sit opposite me on the other couch. I'm religiously fingering the cardboard press credential hanging from my neck.

"Ah," one of them replies.

The two guys across from me nod at my badge: "Media 2006 camp" it says. Beside the little Giants helmet.

"Tiki Barber," the other says.

He is maybe ten years my junior. He is wiry and compact, with black receding hair and a pockmarked face.

"Eric," he says, jabbing his chest with his thumb. He points to his friend on the couch beside him facing out the front window and says, "George." George is baby-faced and younger, with a soul patch and an earring. They nod hello.

"They want Tiki to be a leader in the backfield this season," I say, displaying my credential. "That's what he told me. I sat with him today at lunch. Just him and me. And that's what he told me."

"Tiki," George says, smiling. Everybody smiles when you say "Tiki."

"I'm actually bigger than he is, if you can believe it," I tell them. "It's hard to imagine how he can take such punishment. Know what he told me? He told me playing a game is like running full speed into a brick wall thirty-five times in one afternoon. Most people couldn't even pick themselves off the ground that many times. He says he has a secret, though. Flexible ankles. Don't tell anyone. A lot of people think, Great, he stopped fumbling the ball, and that's the *only* reason he's so productive. But that's not the story. You wanna know what I think is his secret? It's up here."

I tap my temple, raise one eyebrow and give them a "Know what I'm saying?" look. George and Eric smile and nod. All ears.

"Tiki is one of the most thought-out people on the planet. He thinks his way around people. Someone comes up to hit him, but he does this, like, magical telekinesis. He's thought himself past them already . . . if you can conceive of that.

"Tiki told me about one of his great runs. Remember that ninety-five-yarder against Oakland last year? He says that he knew from the moment he broke the huddle and lined up and looked over the defense that if Dave Diehl—that's one of his linemen—could seal off the linebacker, the so-called Mike, Tiki could cut back and go all the way. Tiki was thinking this on his own five-yard line. Taking his stance a yard deep in his own end zone, this is what he's already thinking. D'you understand what I'm saying? A lot of running backs' teeth are chattering against their mouthpiece when they're backed up that far. All they want to do is not get caught in their end zone for a safety. Not Tiki. He's thinking touchdown.

"Tiki is playing and living on a different plane. Oh, he's also fast as hell. I nearly got killed at practice today. Swear to God. I'm watching Tiki run. So on this one play they're practicing he runs to the right, and he cuts in front of where I'm standing. Along the sideline. Full speed. It's amazing how fast they're going. Anyway, the defense is chasing him down . . . and I look up and see there's this one guy coming right at me. Full speed. Right at me. Like a rhino. He's gonna hit me. He can't stop. His name's Chase Blackburn. Linebacker. Coming straight at me. And I'm I'm trying to remember, Did I finish my will yet, know what I mean? The grass is wet and slippery and no way can he stop and he's gonna kill me. That's how close I was standing. But then in just two steps—boom boom, like that—he stops. I thought I was dead. I swear to God. If he ran into me he would've killed me. I wouldn't be sitting here talking to you."

Eric's gaze swings and fastens onto something beyond me out the front window. A bus has pulled up and passengers are coming off. Eric elbows George and their faces split into grins.

"I sorry, I no speak well Englisss," Eric says. He and George jump up and run for the door to welcome the new arrivals, whom I quickly make as compatriots from the way they squeeze their cheeks and smack kisses of greeting on either side of their faces.

The riders pile out of the coach looking gray and pouchy. They look like Eastern European landsmen, tourists who have been sold a one-week package to America, the highlight of which is a gala party in the sumptuous ballroom of the world-famous Clarion hotel in the heart of Albany, America's most exciting city.

Not a one of them speaks a word of English or looks as if he has anything on his mind other than getting ready for the big dance they are apparently holding the next night. The women hoist elaborate ball gowns on hangers slung over their shoulders. They quickly seize control of the washer and dryer in an alcove down the hall from the front desk and begin washing their underwear incessantly, tossing aside the few clothes

I have tumbling around in there without letting them finish their spin cycle.

Their husbands and a few of the children who've been brought along wait beside the bus as the driver gets out and unlocks the luggage door and throws it open. I expect bats to fly out.

In the courtyard outside the university's Indian Quad, where the team eats every day, Shockey stops for a chat en route back to his truck from breakfast. Shockey likes to play football, party and work out, and do you see anywhere in that list where it says *"likes talking to the fucking press"*? No, but today it's the weekend. You know how he feels. He still hasn't gotten all the sleep out of his back muscles. It's quiet. He's got nothing lined up. Birds are chirping. It's a good time for a chat.

The fantastic thing about Shockey is that his essence is uncaged. His soul is permanently on the run from authorities. He shows up for breakfast at camp in his bathrobe. He parties late and comes in game day with a jumbo IV bag of B12. He goes into the weight room and lifts *after* games. Even when he's standing still, or trying to, there ought to be what the cartoonists call motion lines or zip ribbons around him to show movement.

To watch him practice and play football with that sleeve-length tattoo on his right arm is an admonition to your own sagging waistline. But to watch him try to get out of his mouth the same sanitized drivel as most other professional athletes—so free of even a trace of content it will wilt journalists into despair, folding shut their notebooks, letting their microphones drop flaccidly at their hips—is downright funny. He's too authentic.

He is in the practice of adding to the things he does say the endearingly unschooled fillip: "You can write that down." (As if all the reporters were wearing fedoras with little signs saying "Press" tucked in the hatbands.)

On Fridays, before games, the *New York Post* prints Jeremy's pregame comments. The first time I saw this the beer came foaming out of my nose at P. J. Clarke's, where I'd stopped in for a burger and a glance at the papers to get my blood pumping for the weekend. The idea of Shockey, back to an elm, knees drawn up by a brookside, or brandy snifter at his writing table by a crackling fire, dipping pen into ink . . . gathering his thoughts. I had to close the paper.

Giants fans fall into two categories: those who think Mark Bavaro was the greatest tight end in the team's history, and those, like me, who can't look straight at Shockey for an extended period of time for fear of going blind. Outside Giants Stadium, in the celebrative, tailgaters' Giants-ville, among the blue pavilions and grilling meat, the tilting whiskey cups and scavenging seagulls, before any home game, Bavaro is revered, his memory lighting imaginary candles in their minds. He is easily recalled in dark blue silhouette, his relentless bulk carrying tacklers into the end zone and the Giants nation to safety. The quintessential Jersey guy.

But I love Shockey.

Say it: "Shockey."

But wait a second. Just hold on a minute. There's something wrong. Something missing. You can't say the name without an exclamation point at the end, can you? A period won't do. How the hell is a puny period supposed to bring Shockey to a halt? You need an exclamation point to stop it. That's your only hope. Because it's a goddamn runaway word. And the only way it's going to be stopped is by putting a wall in front of it.

Shockey!

The Giants drafted him out of Miami with their first pick in 2002. He made the Pro Bowl his first year and caught 74 passes, setting a team record for tight ends (eclipsing Bavaro's 66, by the way). He entered the league at a time when Philadelphia had ascended to the top of the division along with its young quarterback, Donovan McNabb. McNabb could beat the Giants. He was quick enough to evade Michael Strahan's sacks. The Giants needed a trump card.

Some people, including his current coach, Coughlin, apparently think that Shockey is a constant threat to order. On the contrary. Shockey brings order, moral order, to the team. He plays every play as if it were his last and takes the names of those who make it any harder than it already is.

Shockey!

In a game at Philadelphia in late October of Shockey's rookie season, the Giants' Ike Hilliard was bolting down the left side when then-quarterback Kerry Collins threw him a pass. It was way high, way long, way out of bounds.

But that didn't stop Eagles safety Brian Dawkins. True to the team's eternally cheap and dirty core (if it's true that the former Philadelphia defensive back Andre Waters killed himself last year as a result of brain damage he suffered from so many concussions in the league, perhaps some of the damage came from the dirty hits he regularly delivered to Phil

Simms in the mid-'80s?), Dawkins delivered a running shot at the defenseless Hilliard. His hit broke Hilliard's shoulder and ended his season. It was a cowardly, felonious shot and could not stand unrebuked. Whatever the league office had to say about it after an official review—and it wasn't much, just a fine—the real corrective had to come from down on the field. From the men in the battle.

Who among the fifty-three men who went by the name was Giant enough to exact this revenge?

Three days after Christmas, fighting for a playoff spot in the last game of the season, at home, in the Meadowlands, the Giants faced off in a return match against the division-leading Eagles. Late in the game, deep in Philadelphia territory, Collins was pressured while passing. He tossed the ball wildly up toward the far corner of the end zone.

Jeremy Shockey went up for it. Guarded by Dawkins. They came down together in a heap in the end zone, and Shockey had the rock. While grabbing the ball for a game-tying touchdown (the Giants eventually won in OT), he made sure to slam atop Dawkins with the full force of his 250 pounds, drilling his elbow as deep as possible into Dawkins's solar plexus until it appeared to glance off his backbone like a pickax hitting bedrock. As the official came over to signal touchdown, Shockey took the ball and pasted it to Dawkins's face mask and waggled it back and forth.

"That's for Ike," he said to Dawkins. Then he laughed.

Bavaro wouldn't have done any of that. He would have flipped the ball to the official without saying a word and trotted to the sideline.

Shockey!

"I try to put energy in people. As much as I have," Shockey says in the shade outside the cafeteria, pulling at his morning stubble and nursing a swollen thumb, a souvenir of the previous practice. "That's a thing that you're born with. You know, God gave me that gift."

No wonder Shockey appreciated his first Giants coach, Fassel, "who just really let me go out there and play . . . catch the ball and turn it up the field."

Shockey thinks Coughlin is, quite simply, a "jackass."

"You can write that down."

It rains all afternoon. There is no cover. You get drenched. The rain bangs off you. Shockey lugs around a thumb the size of a cucumber and comes off the line like a getaway car every play.

Chris Mara looks on in a rainproof windbreaker. He has straight, thinning, reddish hair. A friendly, untrammeled look. Chris is the head scout. VP of Player Evaluation. He is shorter and not as pensive-looking as his older brother, who runs the team. His daughter Kate is a successful actress. His wife, Kathleen Rooney, is NFL royalty in her own right as granddaughter of the Steelers' original owner, the legendary Art.

One of the great advantages Chris started off with as a kid is that he didn't need to go to Modell's and fork over $50 to play in a Giants jersey. His dad would bring home a box of old jerseys or discarded uniforms and put it out in the middle of the backyard at the old house in White Plains. (My father never did that for me. To be fair, he made sofa beds, and he couldn't very well have come home one Saturday and piled a bunch of sofa beds in the backyard for me and my brother to fight over.)

"We would call it Mara Stadium," Chris says. "I go by the house now and it's really only about twenty-five yards long. But back then it looked like a hundred. He came home one day and he had a big box of, you know, some of the old jerseys that they had, and he brought it—took it out of his trunk and put it in the backyard and everyone ran and just grabbed them out. And of course I would have been there probably second, and my idol growing up back then was Homer Jones. So I—I got a '45' jersey out of it, which was great. And we put them on and we would play football in our backyard."

I am pelted nonstop, and part of me wants to ask Chris for an umbrella. But holding up an umbrella here on the sidelines would be unfurling some way too overt flag admitting you have pygmy balls. This is football. Fuck rain, mud, cold, ice. Be a man. And, for a moment, as the rain continues to pour down, I begin to feel great. Exhilarated.

I used to play football in the rain all the time. The ecstasy of the mud. Running routes through the puddles. Not caring. Just bouncing around and crashing.

But my excitement fades quickly. Maybe it's just one too many drops falling from my ears. My declining body core temperature. And as my chest-thumping pride melts, the rain focuses the mind on another question as few others things do: "What the fuck am I doing here?"

The last time my cold, damp and creaking bones bedeviled me with this question, it was about 3:15 in the morning at the end of a twelve-hour shooting day in the middle of some woods off a road somewhere outside Vancouver.

I was producing a television show, *Wolf Lake*, that featured a lot of special effects. And now, in the middle of the woods, with everyone exhausted and counting the minutes until they could sack out, we were going to set a man on fire.

The stunt coordinator showed me the cordwood they'd piled into a big mound and how we were going to ignite it in one flash into a huge, flame-licking bonfire reaching up to the branches of the trees twenty feet above us in the darkness. There were gas jets at the base of the pile that we'd fire up on cue.

The fire, the stunt, the gag and what I quickly began to fear might become a horrible accident, maybe even a homicide, here in the middle of nowhere, was the result of a few innocent lines I'd written into a script months earlier back in Los Angeles.

The story was simple enough, and hewed to a reliable formula. Sheriff is told about the crash and explosion of a truck outside town. Sheriff goes to the scene. No truck. Sheriff goes to the hospital looking for the driver. No driver. In fact, Sheriff is told, the driver was picked up and taken from the hospital by a couple creepy-looking guys just moments before Sheriff came looking.

Well, we all know the next beat. Cut right from Sheriff's knitted brow to the hapless truck driver being disposed of so he can't tell anybody what was in that truck he was driving.

My first draft of the scene was too wordy. I turned to my friend Rick. Among his many accomplishments, Rick used to write a lot of comedy material, and once even, to his immortal credit, gave Dean Martin a joke he used at a Friars Club roast for Frank Sinatra. Having Dean Martin use your joke to kill at a roast for the Chairman of the Board is the equivalent of scoring a touchdown in a Super Bowl. The tribute Rick wrote for Dean went something like this: "Frank is a helluva friend. When Sammy Davis Jr. had that car accident and lost an eye, Frank was there. When Joey Bishop didn't have a dime to his name, Frank was there. And when Sammy got all those death threats for marrying a white woman, Frank was there. Frank's a goddamn jinx."

Rick's sage advice was to make the killing-the-truck-driver scene as simple as possible. Forget any buildup. Just cut right to a screaming guy being thrown onto a blazing inferno. Of course. There's your money shot. Go right to it. Then the two guys who throw him on walk out of the shot and are walking back to the truck when the boss stops them. He directs them to look at the conflagration until it has burned the human to ash, with this wonderful line:

"A job worth doing is worth doing well."

Months later, at 3:30 A.M. in the woods outside Vancouver, the irony of that came home to roost as the stunt coordinator approached me from out of the dark, pulling a lanky, stringy-haired guy with him. The stunt coordinator introduced him as his cousin.

"Chuck's gonna be in the bag when we throw it into the fire," he said.

Chuck already looked "in the bag" to me—shiny-faced, eyes unfocused, he looked like he'd just made a deal to help him pay off that night's bar tab.

"Be inside the bag?" I said. "I didn't know we were going to use a real person in there. Can't we just use some weights?"

"The script says he's kicking and hollering," the stunt coordinator said, irritatingly pointing out the words I had written.

"I know what it says," I said, feeling singed by the memory.

" 'Let me out. . . . Hey! . . . Stop!' . . . I've got it memorized," Chuck said, reciting the lines proudly.

"He's a professional," the stunt coordinator said, as we inspected a dark, shapeless sack on the cold ground. It was the body bag they intended to use for throwing Chuck onto the bonfire. "He's done this before. He'll count to five and roll off."

"I'll count to ten," Chuck said, stoutly, and I felt a knot in my stomach tighten.

At this point, the British Columbian provincial fire marshall appeared in the dark, holding the newspaper that he'd canopied over his head to help him catch some shut-eye until an assistant director kicked his chair and awakened him. By law, his presence was required on any set where fire or fireworks were being used.

The fire marshal yawned and dutifully bent and felt the body bag the stunt coordinator had rigged up.

"Feels fine to me," he said.

I wanted to ask Scotland Yard how you could "feel" whether something was flame retardant or not, but he was already tottering back to his chair and the techs were ready to go with the shot. Everywhere people were yawning and heavy-lidded. Everyone wanted to go to sleep, but first we had to set a man ablaze. The director, an amazing, talented, and adept shooter, Tom Wright, was standing by the video assist sizing up the shot. He looked up and said, "Are we ready to go here? Let's do this in one."

Chuck dropped down to the cold ground and somehow folded himself up into that huge duffel and with nary a reassuring word or a fortifying snort of bourbon his cousin, the stunt coordinator, zippered the duffel shut. Two actors, the henchmen in the scene, in the beginning steps of the path they hoped would one day lead to Hollywood's Walk of Fame, grabbed the bag's handles and staggered toward the woodpile.

"Any job worth doing is worth doing well," I kept hearing in my head as they dragged the heavy bundle, stumbling across the dirt. I felt my brain pinch.

Any job worth doing is worth doing well.

How had I gotten here—middle of nowhere in the Canadian woods and about to set a man on fire? Me, Long Island boy and Haverford grad.

"Action!"

Whoomp! A fireball rose and uppercut the forest branches. A red glow flashed across the crew's faces. The flames leaped. The actors, on cue, struggled to heave Chuck onto the inferno.

"There," the director said, watching the video assist as the body bag nestled into the place he'd hoped for the composition of the shot.

I was counting to myself.

"One one thousand . . . two one-thousand . . ."

The flames licked all over the bag, engulfing it. Chuck thumped and struggled within, shouting and doing a stellar, Oscar-worthy job of selling that there was a real, live human being roasting like a pig in there. Wait a second! There was!

I left the video assist and started running toward the fire. I drew up, stopped by a wall of fierce heat.

"Get him outta there," I heard the stunt coordinator yell.

Chuck couldn't roll off the blaze. His bag had gotten hooked on a branch. Grabbing a fire extinguisher, the stunt coordinator quickly killed the flames and his assistants freed the bag, yanked Chuck off the pile, and bumped him to the ground. The body bag was smoking. We tore open the zipper.

Chuck was a little, well, toasty. We could smell where the fire had burned through the flame retardant and begun to scorch his shirt. But another blast from the extinguisher across his back blew out any remaining embers.

The gag worked great. The scene was great. *Any job worth doing is.* . . . well, remember. But I recall thinking, watching the guy burn on the fire I'd created, What the fuck am I doing here? And then realizing suddenly that I was the one inside that bag; I'd put myself in the flames.

Which is exactly what I'm thinking out here by the practice field. I've put myself in the fire again, even though I'm dripping wet and freezing in the Albany rain. I've arranged something too dangerous. Too dependent on details that won't come together. And once you start feeling that way, you kiss off the details. That's the beginning of the end. The first sign of flagging passion. The flicker of the imagination's light.

Why is it about imagination? Because you can't have growth without imagination. The team that's going to win in January is not the team that begins taking snaps in July, it's what that team grows into over the next five months. *That's* the team that will win the championship.

A TV series doesn't start out great, it becomes great. The sixth episode is always better than the second. The second season is better than the first. We know what we're doing now. Here's what works. All components have adjusted, aligned with one another, to locate those things that work best for that canister, so to speak, to contain, when all is said and done, the best film possible. Certain actors play some scenes better than they play others. They may need different prompts. They may best express the point of what you're all trying to achieve in different words. They may work well in certain situations, on certain sets, with or without certain props. And certain types of scenes your company may shoot better than others.

But everyone works toward the same vision.

And the question hovers above every practice and will continue to lurk above every game throughout the season—do Coughlin and his coaches have the vision to write and produce a winning script for their collection of players? I, too, work in a one-hour format, in something that gets filmed, same as sixty minutes of football action, if you will. What, as weird as this sounds, is the best episode of Giants football? That question remained unanswered.

Does this team have the imagination for Jeremy Shockey? Will Coughlin be able to harness Shockey's incredible talent in the most efficient, effective way possible? Will Shockey and his teammates be able to grow, as one, into a championship team? Will they be able, as Archie Manning likes to say, quoting an old coach of his, "to make sure we're all robbin' the same train?"

Years ago I had a beef with the actor Bruce Willis, when he looked at a script I'd given him, saw it called for a lengthy scene in an airplane and told me that he wished the scene rewritten for him to play it alone, in the character's apartment, with nothing but a bottle of Jack Daniel's. "You're robbing me of my gifts," Bruce explained, by confining him in an airplane.

I wonder now if Coughlin isn't doing that very thing to Jeremy Shockey. And I realize that just as I should have swallowed my pride and rewritten the script for Bruce, if this year's Giants are going to coalesce into winners, Coughlin will need to alter the game plan to get the best performance out of Shockey.

At the end of practice I'm soaked to the skin. I trudge with the players off the field and back up the hillside, flanked by young fans screaming for autographs. The players stop and sign before hitting the showers.

I can hardly move. My joints are welded together from two hours of standing, my body clenched against the onslaught of the pouring rain. By my car, in the glen by the towering Escalades, out of sight of the players and the coaches and the sportswriters, I find the driest spot of sod I can and drop down on my back and stretch. *Hnnnnnh!* Leg lifts. *Hnnnnnnh!* Hammy stretches. Something, anything, to make me supple enough to fit back into my rental.

Again: What the fuck am I doing here?

At my training camp headquarters I park under some trees. I remove my sneakers and my socks. I squeeze as much water as I can out of my clothes and hobble across the parking lot toward the Clarion's lobby, trying to not get completely soaked all over again.

Inside, leaving a trail of water, I squish down the long hallway past the elevators toward the alcove with the washer and dryer. I'm shocked and pleased to see an empty dryer, the first I've seen since my fellow Clarion guests arrived on the bus with dirty laundry and no English. I ram what I can into the dryer, then realize I don't have the correct change and head to the desk. I return with a slew of quarters and am in the middle of piling my shirt and socks into the dryer when I realize one terrible, terrible thing: My Giants credential is missing.

I'd taken it off and draped it along with my shirt on the little chair in this cramped room. But it is no longer on the chair. And it isn't on the floor behind the chair. Nor is it behind the dryer. Nor has it been put mistakenly into the dryer.

Standing cold and wet in a shit-bag hotel in Albany, New York, is a good enough reason to scratch your jaw with the barrel of a .38—but being here without my New York Giants credential means definitely pulling the trigger.

I poke my head out into the main hallway. There is a lot of traffic. It seems like everyone in the hotel except for me is getting ready for the celebratory dinner in the ballroom. They scurry on and off the elevators. Women in tight-fitting orange strapless gowns with sequins and faux fur and slits in their dresses you wish someone had sewn up. Men in powder blue tuxedos. All going to a party hosted by some ethnic band, pulsating ting-a-ling music trickling through the doors of the ballroom. Nobody in the hallway is wearing my Giants credential.

"Have you seen a name tag . . . a press credential . . . the one I had around my neck?" I ask at the front desk. For a second I'd thought about going back up to my room, toweling off, getting into dry clothes, and then returning to the lobby to find my credential. But in cases of such import— kidnapping the President's daughter, recovering a purloined Edvard Munch masterpiece, losing my Giants credential— the first sixty seconds are crucial.

Which is why I throw back on my sopping shirt and dart through the partygoers by the ballroom entrance to inquire of the bellman.

But he shakes his head and can only promise, "I'll keep an eye out for it, sir."

I'm more anxious than ever. I run up and down the hall. I check the pool. The stairwell by the annex. Nothing. After a quick scan revealing nothing around the lobby, there remains only one other place I haven't yet looked for my missing credential: beyond the ballroom doors.

They are celebrating some sort of cultural festival devoted to bushy hair, enormous hips, facial moles and ugly clothes, because everyone there has done his or her best to respect as many of these qualities as possible.

Nevertheless, and no matter what they look like, it says something about a man that he can be in a roomful of people cavorting to happy music and not somehow have his spirits raised. It says he's fixated on something. Something that may very well lead to no good. And it is really at this moment, after pushing through the ballroom doors and standing there, squinting hard at the dancers, and listening to whatever nutty foreign-language song the band is so merrily playing, that I feel a chill clench my back and I realize: Shit, uh-oh, I'm in this way too deep, and there's no going back. Me wanting my credential this much is no good.

Still damp, with what I realize are the waters of the Rubicon, I catch sight of my credential. Two kids—maybe eight, maybe ten—are chasing each other around near a grown-up table. There are some other kids tagging along, killing time, looking for mischief. But the one upon whom my gaze alights wears my Giants credential, with its perfectly drawn blue helmet, around his neck.

He must've stuck his head in the washer-dryer alcove and swiped the nice plastic necklace. If he is as football-savvy as the rest of the gathering, there is no doubt he doesn't have the vaguest idea what it is. It was just something that was going to help him kill the next three boring hours. Playing with it, twirling it like a new toy.

"That's mine," I say abruptly, pointing to the credential with the Giants helmet and holding out my hand for him to give it over.

He looks up at me with more fear in his eyes than I'd intended to provoke. But he doesn't say a word. I think he knows what I am talking about. At least knows it isn't really his. And knows I know where he's filched it. So, without a word, he pulls the cord over his head and drops the credential into my palm.

I show the guy at the front desk that I've gotten my credential back and am standing at the elevator doors waiting for them to open when the kid from whom I'd retrieved my prize pokes his head around the corner leading to the ballroom. And he, a second later, is followed by the full figures of two grown men with sweaty faces who look unhappy at having been pulled off the dance floor.

The elevator door opens as the kid points at me, as if to say, There's the mean man who took my toy.

The men whisper to each other. One of them raises his hand at me and yells, "SHTAWP!"

He launches himself toward me. He is a burly man, lineman-big. His arms churn and his tuxedo jacket flaps open, revealing a gold paisley vest. He sports those shiny, slippery tux rental shoes, so he is taking three strides for every two he makes.

I get on the elevator and hit 8.

When he yells "Shtawp!" again it sounds a little angrier. I hear another pair of footsteps thundering behind him. Maybe more than another pair.

If these guys are as drunk as they appear to be, and if they are as pissed off at missing the polka as they appear . . .

I press 8 again.

I didn't steal anything from that kid.

I press 8 again.

It's my credential, I remind myself as I press 8 several hundred more times. In no more than two seconds several large, pissed-off men in rented tuxedos are going to charge into the elevator cabin and slam me so hard my back will splinter.

The doors close on them. One smacks his heel into the door, yelling, "Ey!"

His pal yells something that sounds like "I keel you," and a thrill courses through my veins as my credential and I are aloft and on our way.

And so I head up to safety, clutching my Giants credential. But I am nagged by an intruding thought: This isn't really safety at all, is it? I've just zippered myself up into a burning body bag.

No, I wasn't rising—in fact, I was plunging, falling. Maybe not into a love affair, but into something almost equally irresistible, the way later in life someone returns to religion, surprising and even disappointing those who thought they knew him as a more enlightened man, a purebred product of reason. What my obsession with the Giants shares with religion is the comfort of being part of a flock. But as my credential and I ascend, I am gnawed by the fear that I'm not clutching a ticket to heaven. Far from it. What I've given myself up to, I fear, will offer no salvation.

None at all.

Chapter 3

The Lost City of the Giants

How good would it look on a winter Sunday? One of those clear blue skies with a pat of buttery sun and no wind. Or maybe the weather's turned. The ice floes are trooping downriver. An inhospitable northwest blast, squadrons of white-gray clouds in a fly-by above. How good would Giants Stadium look if it had been built in Manhattan rather than a swamp in New Jersey? How good would it look, looming like a colossus above the piers—the blue, tilted *GIANTS STADIUM* sign gazing solemnly westward out across the Hudson River?

Christ! Instead: All that thumb-wrestling about the West Side stadium. The governor. The mayor. That inbred twerp Dolan from Cablevision, stomping his size 7 feet. Dolan's water carrier, Al D'Amato. The unions. They said it would help the unions. They said it would hurt the unions. They said it would

Sam Huff: Did he leave it all on the field or did the field leave it all on him? NEIL LEIFER

help business. They said it would hurt business. They said it would help the neighborhood. They said it would kill it.

And the Council member from West Giza objected that building such a large pyramid would make camel traffic unbearable.

I fucking ask you: How great would it be?

We would come for brunch right here, P. J. Clarke's. Right on Fifty-fifth and Third. Me and a few friends. Fred. Guy. The Dog. Stanley. Assorted members of the Royal and Ancient Mahmoud Faust Club. After a few and some time spent chatting up the ghosts of Well and Jack Mara, of Steve Owen and John Lummus (who died on Iwo Jima), Frank Gifford and Cliff Livingston and Andy Robustelli and Sam Huff, of Emlen Tunnell and Lawrence Taylor and, God bless him, Fred Exley, the team's Homer, author of the classic *A Fan's Notes*, we'd traverse Manhattan to the new Giants Stadium on the Hudson.

Then we'd have the great and high honor and privilege of watching the Giants come out of the tunnel. (If you don't know what I mean, go to Amsterdam, buy a ticket to the Rijksmuseum and plant yourself in front of *The Night Watch*.)

But apparently the Maras are content among the liquor store owners from Tenafly and the industrial park prols from Plainfield. The Giants and Jets have gone in together on a billion-and-a-half-dollar, brand-new joint out in the Meadowlands, and they got hundreds of millions of dollars of loans from the league to build it. This new stadium—to be ready, they say, by 2010—is a sure sign that neither team is coming back: Your erstwhile neighbor leaves, rents in another town and builds there.

Most performers seek the acclaim of the best audiences, which means a New York stage and not the Hackensack Playhouse. In 1991, resolving a bitter feud between Wellington and the family of his late brother Jack, half the franchise was sold to Bob Tisch (who died weeks after Wellington). The Tisches are showbiz folk. Bob's son Steve is a hugely successful, Oscar-winning movie producer whose films include *Pursuit of Happyness*, *Forrest Gump* and *Risky Business*. Didn't Steve clear the family throat and say, "Fellas, we had some of our greatest designers and builders come up with a few models of a Hudson site stadium we think you ought to at least look at before booking us into a fucking peat bog, how about it?"

I'm sure Fred Exley would agree with me on this. I met him twenty years ago out in Pasadena. We were going to watch our favorite team play in its first Super Bowl. He was the same age as I am now. His indignity-inflicted frame had gone from baguette to puff pastry. He had, by his own word, lived much of life inert and doing next to nothing in the way of caloric conversion, balanced on bar stools at, among other places, P. J. Clarke's, or adhered to patio davenports, sparking cigarettes, downing what he called Vodka Presbyterians. Life, it appeared, offered him little, but on his mad journey he remained faithfully tethered to his hometown of Watertown, New York, and to one other thing: the affairs of a professional football team named the Giants.

It was chaotic outside the rounding brick façade of the Rose Bowl looming before us. The *WHOCK-WHOCKING* echoes of the media choppers overhead seemed to unnerve Exley. He looked up at the brick and stopped as if he had remembered something. Maybe it was the memory of being inside the Rose Bowl once before when he was just a kid, a student at USC the same time his idol Frank Gifford was, and getting drunk and sneaking inside and romping around the deserted field when no one was there. Or perhaps he was reminded of other brick walls within which he'd been forcibly confined and electroshocked. Whatever, he dug in his heels against the chaos.

Fred Exley stood outside the Rose Bowl in Pasadena on January 25, 1987, just before his team was to play the Denver Broncos for a championship they'd last won in 1956 and announced he wasn't going in. I didn't believe my ears.

Exley clutched in his hand a screwdriver and the Super Bowl ticket Frank Gifford had given him. We were shuffling toward one of the long, dark narrow entrance tunnels. He took one step toward a postage-sized stamp of daylight that was barely visible at the egress end of the passage, and his forehead broke into beads of queasy, claustrophobic sweat.

"I can't go in there," he said, looking as if he'd come to the banks of the Styx.

"Sure you can. It'll be okay. It's the only way in."

"Maybe I'll watch the game at a bar," Exley said. "I'll get a cab." He looked around as if we were standing at the corner of Fifty-fifth and Third outside P. J. Clarke's, and not Pasadena, where cabs didn't just come cruising by.

"We're right here. Frank Gifford himself gave you a ticket. You wanna see the Giants win the Super Bowl, don't you, Ex? Of course you do. That's the whole point. That's why we're here. . . ."

But he stood back. In a moment Fred Exley was stranded there, free of our clutches. We were borne along in the crowd surge toward the game. I caught a final glimpse of him, looking small and frail. He never made it in. I remember wondering with dismay: How much stomach could a man lose before something as great as this didn't count for anything anymore?

How could a man give up a ticket to watch the Giants play in the Super Bowl?

I found that out for myself.

"If that guy Silver, that politician who vetoed the project . . . if he was sitting over there right now . . . y'know what I'd do? I'd go over there and dump the rest of this omelet on his head."

The bartender at P. J.'s listens to my imaginary set-to with the Speaker of the New York State Assembly, and responds, somewhat irritably, "The West Side stadium was gonna be for the Jets, anyway."

"Yeah, well, the Giants were thinking about moving there," I say. "If it was up to me they would."

Will you listen to me? What's that growl in my voice? That defensive serration lately? I'm touchy. What in my life has changed so suddenly to get me so on edge? At first I thought, Wait a second, nothing's changed—money worries, mortgage worries, will worries, wife worries, kid worries . . . 'ey, I'm pulling the usual train. Over the usual terrain: the perpetual ignorant drift of the world, across whose waters I scale the things I write and watch them, finally, disappear beneath the waves after however many skips. Then I realized, Of course, I've hitched on a new boxcar: Giant worries.

Weeks into my season-long odyssey I sit in bed at night, reading, or trying to read, philosophy—Leo Strauss or Isaiah Berlin or other things I think it important to read, like the Koran, or maybe one of those big histories about the Revolutionary War period, something that a week ago I was devouring with relish, powering through all the footnotes, generating a mini-windstorm by flip-flopping the pages back and forth to the maps and then to the chapter notes and the military campaigns, when suddenly I'll leave George Washington to drown in the Delaware and begin wondering how Tiki Barber's thumb is.

Maybe I get as far as brushing my teeth after I wake up in the morning before I glance up into the mirror and think, I wonder if a good night's sleep helped Tiki's hand.

A guy at another bar recently didn't turn on the game fast enough and for some reason about five minutes later the manager came over to me and asked me to leave, claiming I had used loud and abusive language. He might have been right.

I'm not sure I see the benefit of all this. At first it was just twitching in bed at night. Now it has progressed from the unconscious to thinking about them all day. Thinking about their schedule, the games, the matchups. It is such useless information, filling your mind with agate type when it should be set on loftier affairs, like Leo Strauss's collected lectures on the principle of natural right. Or even just more important things, like, say, paying for my kid's education and, speaking of which, she wants to change schools and there's a complex, pain-in-the-ass application process to go through that's sure to incite family torment. Thinking about my daughter's future would at least be time put to better use than worrying about the things you worried about when you were nine years old, like whether or not to bring an extra pair of sneakers to the game on Sunday and whether or not the world would end if the Giants lost.

These are the same Giants worries I had as a kid. They're there for me to touch, there to make me pretty much fucking deaf to nearly everything else in the world—the agents, the networks, the pitches, the scripts, the back end. Life, it turns out, has simply grown in around the Giant worries. Obligations have crowded them out and overpowered them to the ground, where they mingle with dust.

Nevertheless there's a weird elation, one intoxicating whiff you could get, like from rolling a dead leaf or a cigar, of a lost world that's still there: me.

"I'm not a moron, you know," I say to the bartender at P. J.'s.

"Huh?" he says, leaning forward, cocking his ear.

"The Giants should have built the stadium there."

This comes out sounding a little belligerent. The bartender gives me an "I've got better things to do" look, so I take one last stab at explaining myself:

"Picture it. The new Giants Stadium. Mara Field. The snow coming down . . . the Giants driving for the winning touchdown. Late in the game . . ."

"Don't hold your breath, my friend," the bartender says, cutting me off, pivoting away from me the way, let's face it, people have been doing for the last few months.

Although my wife has told me to mind myself, I've begun seizing control of any conversation left dangling in the air for a moment to talk about the Giants and Mark Ingram's great play against the Buffalo Bills in Super Bowl XXV.

The bartender doesn't have to remind me I live in the lost city of the Giants. Maybe traces of the lost city of the Giants can be found via NASA satellite photos, the way archaeologists located the ancient city of Iram in Arabia, the Atlantis of the Sands, the former capital of the spice route (great pictures in *National Geographic*, by the way).

Satellites can show the outlines of things that used to exist. Not all of the places. But maybe you could still see where some things were. Maybe it would show how it was at the place I'm at now, P. J. Clarke's, before the team left Yankee Stadium, when you could drain your Jameson, hop on the el and be in your seat in twenty-seven minutes. It might show Toots Shor's. It would show the remains of the old Polo Grounds, where, on December 7, 1941, my father and mother were sitting, watching the Giants lose, while it was Tora! Tora! Tora! halfway around the world at Pearl Harbor, and where Wild Bill Donovan (America's top spy) was so interested in the game he held off taking an emergency long-distance phone call to watch one final play—the Dodgers' Pug Manders diving into the end zone to put Brooklyn up by two touchdowns on Hinkey Haines Day— *TUFFY LEEMANS* ? before, realizing the game was a lost cause, he picked up the phone. It was Jimmy Roosevelt calling from the White House, telling Donovan the President needed to see him immediately.

The satellite might show the outlines of the old American Radiator Building on West Fortieth Street, where, one day in November of 1926, in a promotional stunt arranged by Tim Mara, Lynn Bomar tossed a pass from the roof to Hinkey Haines, who was standing in Bryant Park, 324 feet below. The first pass hit the sidewalk and burst. The next two went wild. The fourth knocked Hinkey ass over teakettle, but he held on to the fifth.

There'd be the Maras' apartment at Park and Seventy-eighth, and the team's old headquarters at Columbus Circle, where Tim, spurning all the good PR he'd get with a big Giants sign and office, insisted the team work out of the second floor. He had a lot of cash on hand from ticket sales and was always afraid having a place on street level was asking to get robbed. Outside, on the street of my lost Giants city, Gunther Toody drives by in a squad car.

The Lost City includes the still-standing Roosevelt Hotel, home of Tim Mara's old Turf and Gridiron Club, whose membership rolls counted three New York governors. And from there it runs across Forty-second Street to the old Knickerbocker Hotel, where Tim Mara had a gaming operation for putting bets on ponies and fights.

And the subway station beneath it at the southeast corner of Times Square. I wandered over there a few months ago on a steamy midsummer night, standing in the subterranean churn of human haste, asking a female transit cop if she'd let me go out on the platform for free.

"Why should I do that?" she said, looking severely disinclined. Her long black fly-away hair was pasted to her neck from the sweat.

"I'm looking for something at the end of the platform," I said. "An old sign over a private entrance."

"There is no private entrance here," she said. "This is the only entrance."

I pointed up the stairs to the gray glimmer of the street. It had begun to rain and the drops sprayed off the heels of the scurrying riders.

"You know that building up there?"

"You mean the Gap," the lady cop said.

"It used to be a hotel. A grand hotel built by one of the Astors. Where the martini was invented. There used to be a private entrance from the hotel to the subway somewhere down here."

Finally, she waved me through, but kept a close eye lest I suddenly pull an envelope full of anthrax grains from my blazer, leaving her with a killer amount of paperwork to do.

It wasn't far down the platform, but there it was. The

locked-up door that opened onto the stairway leading to the basement lobby of the Knickerbocker Hotel. The sign above it, *KNICKERBOCKER*, grimy and stained and dull, yet not at all hard to read after eighty years without so much as a bell-hop's sleeve to polish it.

"The traces left by past events never move in a straight line," the French historian and martyr Marc Bloch wrote, "but in a curve that can be extended into the future." Standing here, I imagine how the Giants started. Right here. Eighty years ago. Through this doorway. Out of which, one spring day in April of 1925, came Tim Mara, thirty-eight, leaving his office upstairs in the Knickerbocker and in a hurry to get crosstown.

He is a "large, curly-headed, thick-fleshed Irishman with the wide, relaxed, dimpled, big-mouthed, and keen type of Irish face," as described by James Agee a decade later in *Fortune* magazine.

Mara's just shrugging his topcoat down over his big shoulders as he bolts out the door and onto the busy subway platform. He catches a shuttle east to Grand Central. The long blocks on 42nd Street that stretch between Mara's office on the second-floor mezzanine of the Knickerbocker and Grand Central Station at the other end of the line are where America plays, parties, gambles, dances, and sings and writes about it. A block away, Will Rogers stars in *The Ziegfeld Follies*. Fred Astaire and his sister, Adele, star in George Gershwin's *Lady, Be Good* at the Liberty Theater. Jack Dempsey is the heavyweight champion of the world.

Mara emerges from the subway at Grand Central and heads for the office of Billy Gibson, a fellow sportsman. Gibson, almost fifty, is a slender, rakish boxing manager. Mara has frequented Gibson's bar in East Harlem—the Toots Shor's of its day—and Gibson's Fairmont Athletic Club, a small boxing venue housed in an old foundry at 251 East 137th Street near Third Avenue in the South Bronx. This is where one summer night in 1916, legendary sportswriter Grantland Rice watched the young Dempsey fight and dubbed him "the Manassa Mauler."

But the subject for Mara and Gibson today is another fighter who has designs on Dempsey's title: Gene Tunney (whose name Mara always pronounced *tooney*, like *took*). He is, like Mara, an Irish kid from Greenwich Village.

Gibson is Tunney's manager. They are crusading for Dempsey's title. But Dempsey isn't defending any titles. Following his wild victory over Luis Firpo in 1923 (you can see George Bellows's famous painting of the fight at the Whitney), Dempsey has allowed himself to be matched in defense of his title only once in the past couple years, against Harry Wills, in Jersey City, on September 6, 1924.

Mara and Gibson and everyone else know what happened in that fight: nothing. It never came off. Tex Rickard, the promoter, had canceled it. The stated reason was fear of racial unrest. Wills was black. And Rickard had no intention of watching the heavyweight crown pass from the hands of white America, which had reclaimed it from Jack Johnson following no small national tumult a decade and a half before.

Gibson and Tunney—and Mara—saw their chance to move into the breach. Mara was calculating the steep price he was going to charge for that help as he bolted out of his digs at the Knickerbocker and onto the subway that morning and made his way to Gibson's office.

Gibson didn't fear Dempsey, he feared New Jersey boxing rules. Fights in New Jersey did not end on scorecards, they ended either with KOs or no decisions if each man had answered every bell.

Tunney brimmed with confidence, but neither he nor his manager nor his friend Mara thought he could knock out the ferocious Dempsey. His best odds at becoming champion would be to fight Dempsey in a state where the title could be won on points. Like New York. That's where it had to be.

"The Boxing Licensing Commission absolutely refuses to license Dempsey to fight us here," Gibson confirms to Mara once he's come in and gotten out of his coat and they've got the pleasantries out of the way. This is the thorn in their side: The three-member commission, voting 2–1, announced that the only Dempsey fight it would sanction was against Wills, "the Black Panther," who'd been unfairly denied his shot six months before.

Gibson says he knows what good friends Tim is with Governor Al Smith. Maybe some evening over a nice roast cooked by Mrs. Mara or out somewhere at one of those tedious black-tie functions, Tim could put in a word and ask his friend Smith to intervene and overrule the commission.

It sounds easy. But Mara, oddsmaker that he is, knows it's more of a long shot than that. The swing voter, the man who is, in effect, vetoing the Dempsey-Tunney fight in New York, is James Farley. And Farley has an even bigger match in mind: pushing his man, Al Smith, to the Democratic presidential nomination and the White House over the next three years, in 1928. He will need New York's African-American vote to do that, and he won't get it if Al Smith sells out a black man who is clearly the top contender, and spreads out the welcome mat for Dempsey and Tunney.

Mara tells Gibson his price: He wants a quarter of Tunney's purse and future earnings if he succeeds with the governor. Onion-eyed and high-waisted, Billy Gibson is probably still cackling at his young pal Mara's gall when his secretary buzzes to say his luncheon appointment has arrived. She shows in two men who've just gotten off the train from the Midwest: a bespectacled sportswriter from Columbus, Joe Carr, and his friend, Dr. Harry March.

Gibson introduces them to Tim Mara, whom they've never before laid eyes on. Gibson has known Carr for years, initially having met him on swings through the Midwest managing his first great fighter, the Jewish lightweight champ Benny Leonard.

Carr wears another hat for this meet, though—he's president of a professional football league, sandlot outfits in shit-shovel midwestern towns whose tallest buildings are silos, like Moline and Rockport. He and March are here to find a backer for a New York franchise, a tent pole around which a ragtag league could build to viability. Gibson is their man.

But Gibson tells Carr and March they've come a long way for nothing. He has his hands full making Tunney a world champ and no time to spare.

"How about Tim?" Gibson asks, turning toward Tim and suddenly filled with delight at his great idea.

"Me?" Mara laughs. He knows everything about horse racing and about boxing—that's his business. But professional football? He's never seen a game.

Confronted by the vast extent of Tim Mara's football ignorance as they were, it's hard to understand how two men who had journeyed so far, with a proposal so important to the future of their enterprise, could so blithely pin their hopes on a man they'd never met whose only recommendation was that he happened to be standing next to the guy who just told them to get lost. You could piss out the window and hit someone who knew more about football than Tim Mara.

There was another, major reason to hesitate: Mara's game—bookmaking. "Bookmaking," however legal it was, carried certain negative connotations since the 1919 Black Sox World Series, which had been fixed by gambler Arnold Rothstein, someone with whom Gibson was well acquainted. Rothstein (Scott Fitzgerald named him Meyer Wolfsheim in *The Great Gatsby*) was assisted in the Black Sox scandal by Abe Attel, the ex-boxer. Attel was a pal of Mara's and Gibson's, and ran a joint a couple blocks away that was a swell place to eat lunch, and it figured that the two guys just off the train from Ohio must be starving.

"You can use my name if it'll help," Gibson tells Carr and Dr. March, looking to close the deal. "I'll be president of the football franchise, but Tim's got to put up the money. What do you say, Tim?"

Gibson's loving this moment, enjoying pinning a price tag on young Mara's vest. Turning the tables on him. Mara had waltzed in looking for a quarter of Tunney's purse and has gone from brash to clueless in five minutes. Doesn't have the vaguest idea what's a fair price for a football franchise. You could say fifty bucks or fifty thousand; he wouldn't know. Besides, Gibson thinks he knows how much of a shot pro football has in New York—none. Zero. He'd sunk some money into a team a couple years ago and lost every penny. You had to be the town idiot to invest so much as a nickel of your money in professional football.

"So what do you say, Tim?" Gibson asks.

"By the way, how much does a franchise go for?" Mara finally gets around to asking, doing his best to conceal his ignorance.

Carr says the price for a franchise in the two-year-old National Football League is $500. Mara purses his lips.

"Five hundred for a franchise for anything in New York's gotta be a good deal," Mara says with a shrug as Billy Gibson manages to keep a straight face.

In five years, glinting-eyed Billy Gibson won't be the fight game's top manager anymore, won't be playing golf at Winged Foot every Sunday. Instead, he will be bankrupt and declared legally insane. Not that many years hence, Tim Mara's franchise will be worth almost a billion dollars simply because Tim did a little back-scratching that day.

Returning to his Knickerbocker office that afternoon, Tim Mara's mind is occupied planning how to approach his old pal Governor Smith for help with making that match between Dempsey and Tunney. "Oh, yeah," he reminds himself, "I also own a football team."

"Did you see everything you wanted to see?" the lady cop asked me after I pushed my way out through the turnstile.

"Yeah," I said. I thanked her, and continued passing through. "It was right where I thought it would be."

"It's funny," the cop said, pulling her hair away from where it had stuck to her cheek, "I've been working this station for six months and I've never noticed it."

"You have to like the job Lovie Smith is doing. . . ."
   "You have to love what LT brings to the table. . . ."

"You have to be concerned about this team's ability to rush the passer. . . ."

"You have to think that somewhere deep down the fans are thinking it's time for a change. . . ."

The pregame for some other football game is on the TV at P. J.'s. It would be easy to mock Howie and Jimmy and Michael and Steve and Terry and Tony and Boomer and all the rest of the guys who form one slice of the big, fat multi-billion-dollar pie Tim Mara put in the oven back when. But the disgusting truth is, I love them. There's no accounting for it. Once, recently, while I was watching one of the endless dozens of blather-and-highlight shows that consume far too many hours of my day, my daughter walked into the room and pointed at my face and said, "Dad, why're you smiling?"

I glanced sideways into the mirror by my bed and saw what she meant. My jaw hung open in a dull, mindless gape and my lips were slack and wet. I recoiled in shock, as if I'd come face-to-face with some other me. And then I realized: I had. This was the me of the future. Me in my waning days. Pushed into a day-room somewhere. In front of a TV on the wall. A tremor in my hand that makes me take ten minutes before I can zero in on that place on the side of my nose to scratch. That same smile on my face. Watching the Giants' pregame. Or maybe that Friday-night cable equivalent of the great French Enlightenment salon at Madame de Lambert's that we call, nowadays, *Giants Online*.

"You've got to admire Coach Reid for the way he's kept this team together. . . ."

"You've got to love the way this kid runs his routes. . . ."

"You've got to think ball control is going to be a big part of their game plan today. . . ."

It's still early in the season, but all day Sunday is taken up watching pre-and-postgame commentary on every TV I can find, including here at P. J.'s. It's still pretty warm, too, but soon enough, presumably, out on the street men in work gloves will offload trucks laden with the first Christmas trees of the season. They are the best-looking. Vernal. Healthy, green and six, seven feet high and broad at the base. Up and down Third Avenue. You can smell the sweet pine scent blowing off the bristles even before you have finished brunch and taken care of the check.

"So you goin' to the game today?" the bartender asks me when it's time to settle the bill.

"Yeah," I say. I dig into my pocket for some money. I pull out a stray ten dollars and flourish it. "Gotta save this for the round trip to the swampland. Do you believe how stupid it is, not building that new stadium right here on the West Side? But I know: 'Don't hold my breath.'"

"Oh. That's not why I said, 'Don't hold your breath,'" the bartender says. "I meant Manning. Don't hold your breath for Manning."

"What's the matter, you don't like Eli Manning?"

The bartender shrugs. "He's not his brother."

"What's that supposed to mean?"

He shrugs again. What more explanation did I want? You could say the same thing about Jimmy and Billy Carter. About Bill and Roger Clinton. About Richard and Donald Nixon. One of the two falls short.

"He's not his brother."

He may be the second greatest Manning in the NFL today, but he's my Manning. BILL FRAKES

Chapter 4

Cain, Abel, and Eli

The last time I ever really saw my father, we were watching football. Not at the game. We were watching on TV. This was in November some years ago in his hospital room at Mount Sinai. He'd had valvoplasty performed a couple days before, and then incurred a painful aneurysm at the site. It kept him bedded down for a few days.

I was the co-executive producer of the TV series *Mad About You*. I was in the middle of writing a script, and finding it even more of a challenge than usual to be funny or even helpful. I flew to New York to spend the afternoon with him. And to watch the game.

It was the way we usually watched. Not much talking. My father would either pronounce "Man alive" when a player made a good tackle or a catch, or "Unbelievable!" when he didn't. Then, just before halftime, my father said something else a bit more cryptic: "I think I should tell you that the train is coming."

"What?" I said. I heard him, but it made no sense.

"I'm simply trying to inform you. The train is coming," he said in a very even, logical voice, waiting for me to catch on to the truth of what he was saying, or at least trip over it. He nodded over my shoulder. But not at the TV screen. "Don't you see it? I'm right in the middle of the tracks."

All I saw was the Giants being stopped for no gain.

"There are no tracks here, Dad. We're in the hospital."

"Nevertheless," he said, and he looked at the spot over my shoulder. "I tell you, it's coming straight for me."

I realized that my father wasn't seeing the Giants game from his hospital room in the intensive care unit on 101st Street the day before he was set to leave the hospital. Instead, he was back on Long Island staring up the eastbound track from our Long Island Rail Road Station at Center Avenue. Ours was a stop on the Long Beach spur that diverged south from the Babylon line after Lynbrook. Every day, the train brought my father home from work at King Sleep, at 45 East 20th Street, where he made sofa beds.

The train descended a mile-long low grade in a straight line, gathering immense momentum. It rushed through the crossing with the lights flashing and the bell clanging furiously until it somehow came to a stop and the air brakes gasped and my father would emerge, another day checked off.

"There's no train coming, Dad. Just watch the Giants game. Maybe they'll get a first down."

"It's heading right for me, I'm simply trying to tell you," he said. "I'm right in the middle of the tracks."

Within minutes—moments—my father's face bubbled purple with rage and he began cursing me.

"You no-good son of a bitch. Don't you see it!"

I was told later the dementia was the first sign of what was happening. Infection had unleashed an edematous torrent of fluid into his lungs.

"You rotten little bastard," he railed, "I'm right in the middle of the tracks. I ask you to help me, you good-for-nothing son of a bitch. . . . I can't breathe, I tell you. I can't breathe. . . . Fuck you, you rat . . . you no-good little son of a bitch. . . ."

Nurses hurried forth. My father's chest heaved. I understood the fight, the primal, panicky fight for air; I had asthma as a child. I was told to step back from my father. They pulled a curtain around him and pushed in a rattling cart. And, shortly, they tugged back the curtain and it slid aside on its track, to reveal my father, intubated and unconscious; and, though he lingered for a cruelly long six more months, he was, right there, in the middle of the Giants game, gone. The man who made the sofa beds. Claimed by King Sleep. He'd seen the train coming. He'd been right.

I think of my dad when I journey to games. He was a man who loved nothing better than "to work up a good sweat" playing sports. And whenever I couldn't sleep at night, he'd sit on the edge of my bed and sing "Annie Laurie," as well as James Dunn sings it in the film of *A Tree Grows in Brooklyn*, and tell me to put everything else out of my mind and just think of a good play I'd made, a touchdown catch, or a good hit, and that would bear me off to peaceful, contented sleep.

The round-trip bus fare to the Meadowlands from Port Authority is nine bucks. It's surprisingly comfortable and quick. If you can't exactly pub-crawl to it or, almost as good, take a subway, at least it's urban mass transit of a sort, and you're along for the ride with others whose hearts, for the most part, are in the right place.

Unfortunately, most of them, unlike me, want their hearts back from Eli Manning. The team has had him since around the time we invaded Iraq, and right now the war and the younger Manning seem best characterized by the same two things: mission not accomplished, and high-level bureaucrats reaffirming a confidence not shared by the constituency.

Not his brother.

Not his brother. . . .

If you're a little brother no one's ever happy, right on down to the bartender at P. J. Clarke's. Your life is always an "if." Your life is always "compared to." Always what was better than or not as good as. Could have. Might have. Didn't.

Little brothers face an inhospitable world. We've earned the right to live as long as we understand we'll never measure up. As long as everybody can agree to that, okay, sit down, you can eat.

If my father was Archie, the All-American quarterback, and my brother was Peyton, the quote under my photo in the high school yearbook would be something like: "Get that goddamn football out of my face."

But Eli followed the footsteps. There's enough Gothic in the family genome to put a pen in the hands of Tennessee Williams. Father Archie. Small-town Mississippi boy. The summer after his freshman year at Ole Miss, returning home from a family celebration, Archie is the first to find his father's body, a suicide from a shotgun. His mother says, We'll get by somehow at home, son, you go back to school. Reluctantly, he does. His father never sees Archie become an All-America quarterback at Ole Miss, where the campus speed limit to this day—thirty-five years after he last took a snap for the Rebels—is seventeen miles an hour in honor of Archie's jersey number. Archie marries the Homecoming Queen, Olivia Williams. Sixteen years a pro, the symbol of the New Orleans franchise. Never quarterbacked a winner and calls his career "unfulfilled."

He has three sons. The oldest, Cooper, goes to Ole Miss also, but chooses different shoes: not as a quarterback, as a receiver, the person at the opposite end of the pass. Cooper's career is cut short by injury. The next son, Peyton, decides he will be a quarterback, only he won't go to Ole Miss. Peyton goes to Tennessee, pissing off everyone in the state of Mississippi, and fulfills every professional expectation one could have for one's boy. Becomes the Colts QB. Is already being touted as possibly "the greatest quarterback in history," which is what Frank Gifford called him before he heard himself saying it and stopped himself short.

The third son, the runt of the litter, decides he too will be a quarterback. At the same high school—Newman, in New Orleans—as Peyton. Doesn't duck his dad's alma mater the way Peyton did, but embraces it. Becomes an All-America QB at Ole Miss like his pop and a top overall draft pick like his brother.

This is not what little brothers are supposed to do. Historically, after all, the little brother is usually disinherited from the family business, whether it's landholding or pro quarter-backing. The younger carves his own ill-starred path, racing on two wheels on life's Grande Corniche far above the casino, where he has, like the prodigal son, gambled it all away and disgraced the family name. He becomes, ultimately, an antic, self-hating entrepreneur who trades on popularity and suffers the lacerating fate of cursing himself with what he has felt cursed by all along: that there is, in fact, nothing in his name for him.

His destiny is to become nothing, to become unrecognizable to his family, maybe the way I was to my father as he cursed me from his hospital bed. Eli, though, may be too frightened by the idea of making himself unrecognizable to his family. The only way he may succeed in making himself unrecognizable to his family is by being a lousy quarterback.

Perhaps Eli will be an "if" forever. But he has arranged it so that the question "Will he ever be as good as his brother?" will follow Eli to the football grave. We're supposed to get an answer right away this season, in the opening game that NBC is calling "the Manning Bowl," Colts against Giants from the Meadowlands.

I tried to gauge Archie's take on his sons' parallel football careers months before the season even started but just after the league had published the schedule and people had taken a gander, risen from their Barcaloungers and cracker barrels, screeched their pickups to a halt in the yard, turned off the motor and the radio, raced through the screen door into the kitchen, and hunted down a pen and X'ed the date on their wall calendars when the two brothers would meet in battle. I had a theory that Eli needed one of two things to become a better quarterback. Either Eli had to win that first game of the season or Peyton had to win the last game of the season. Either Eli had to overcome Peyton in the Manning Bowl opener, announce right away he could no longer be defined as not as good as his big brother, or, the next best thing, Peyton had to win the Super Bowl, get that monkey off his back, step aside and let Eli have his turn without feeling guilty about it.

Archie and I split a plate of fried crawfish at Landry's, hard by the levee in the French Quarter. It was early spring, a few months after Hurricane Katrina. The city was razed. But Archie was back at his home in the largely untouched, well-off Garden District, invoking smiles and greetings from passersby as he strolled through "the sliver by the river." If you imagine how tough to take you'd be if you were Archie Manning and you were the greatest football stud of all time, you can startle yourself with the realization of just what a humble and unassuming man he is. If the South issued its own postage stamps, Archie Manning's face would be on one.

He wasn't worried about how Peyton and Eli would handle the Manning Bowl.

"Peyton and Eli aren't going to start yelling at each other about who can do this and who can do that," he said. "They'll compete. It won't change their relationship any. They'll deal with it."

Archie recalls being at the Meadowlands when Eli made his first appearance in Giants blue back in 2004. It was a game against Philadelphia, a typical no-holds-barred, kill-or-be-killed rumble that ends one lick shy of a call to the coroner's office. Eli came off the bench to replace the injured starter, Kurt Warner. Eli called a play, retreated to pass, began to scramble and was blindsided by defensive tackle Jerome McDougle. He was knocked silly.

"[Green Bay Packers quarterback] Bret Favre told me that was the hardest lick he's ever seen," Archie said. "I was sitting in the stands with my wife and when Eli went down, Olivia dug her fingernails into my thigh and she said, 'You think he's all right?' And I thought to myself, All right? I just hope Eli's not dead. I thought he'd killed him. I wasn't sure he was going to get up. I mean, those guys are trained killers."

Two things made a lasting impression on Archie that day: his youngest son Eli's getting up, and his wife Olivia's fingernails.

"Baby steps . . . baby steps," Archie kept drawling, cautioning patience for Eli's development. He has deep-set blue eyes and retains the gaze of a quarterback, looking downfield, taking in what may be in store and what's got to be done about it. "It's tough in New York. Those six days between games in New York are tougher than any other place. If you win, they go too fast. If you lose, the next game never comes around again. And it can be double bad with all the media in New York. The good thing about Eli is he doesn't pay too much attention either way."

It turns out Archie's got the same deal trying to figure out Eli like the rest of us do, and he's been at it way longer. Since Eli was born, while Archie was finishing his career up in Houston and Minnesota, so that he didn't have the "stroller time" with Eli back home in New Orleans. Archie remembers Eli as so quiet that when the kid's friends called the house and Archie answered, he was never sure if Eli was home or not, because he heard no sounds, no loud music or foot-stomping, coming from upstairs.

Is anything going on up there? is what we're *all* wondering.

All Giants fans have the same impulse: We want to get inside Eli's head, psychoanalyze the kid, find some hitherto masked interiority. Find what makes him tick and tune him up so he avoids those episodes of wavering resolve, distracted decision making and wayward passing.

I imagine ushering him into my book-lined office in the brownstone off Central Park West. He wears a crew-neck sweater, jeans. Big cowlick. I tell him to take a seat.

"They told me I was supposed to see a Dr. Director," Eli says. "My, my, look at all those diplomas. You must be one hell of a good head shrinker."

"So you have some idea why you're here?" I ask him.

"Not really." He shrugs. "Except Mr. Mara and Mr. Tisch and Coach Coughlin said they'd let me out of practice."

"You're aware that many people are concerned about you, Eli?"

"No, not really."

"The entire city of New York."

"That's nice of them."

"I'm glad you think so. Tell me, have you noticed anything unusual lately?"

"Unusual . . ."

"Sights . . . sounds . . . Like booing. Catcalls."

"No, not really."

"You don't concern yourself too much with that sort of stuff, do you?"

"I just go out there and try to go through my reads . . . find the open man and get him the ball."

"I'm sure you do."

"I think I've got to play better football."

"Good, Eli. We're on the same page about that. Playing better football."

"Going through my reads, finding the open man and making a good throw . . ."

"Good."

"Going through my reads . . ."

"Eli!"

"Yessir!?"

"Forget about the 'reads' for a second. What about the things inside you? Like your feelings?"

"My feelings?"

"Yes. We all have feelings. Sometimes we don't like showing them. Maybe they scare us. Feelings aren't necessarily a bad thing, Eli. They can even be a good thing. If we face them."

"Oh, I know. I have feelings."

"Good, I'm sure you do. Why don't you tell me about your feelings for your brother."

"Peyton or Cooper?"

"Peyton. What are your feelings about him?"

"He's my brother. Those are my feelings. I love my brother."

"Of course, but don't you have any feelings, say, of jealousy?"

"Jealous? Of Peyton?"

"People call him the best quarterback. He sets all the records. He's going to the Hall of Fame. He's just about the coolest white man in America. They'll probably ask him to host *Saturday Night Live*!"

"Mmm . . . Nope. No jealousy."

"I could understand if you did. I'd be jealous."

"He's my brother."

"I was jealous of my older brother because he was a better football player than me. All the girls liked him—"

"Well, like I say, I just gotta go out there and make my reads. . . ."

"Everybody always patting him on the back . . . telling him how good he is . . . Everything he does is the best. . . . How's that supposed to make you feel . . . ?"

"Well, I think if I just go out there and make my reads . . ."

"It feels lousy. Admit it. It sucks. Sometimes you wish to hell the guy was dead, for crying out loud, don't you? And that makes you really hate yourself—"

"—I think I've just got to play better football, Doc—"

"—Exactly what I'm talking about. If you don't let all that out it holds you back. Trust me. Don't internalize it. If you don't examine any of this, then one day, I don't know when . . . say it's a big game against the Eagles. You come out of the huddle to the line of scrimmage. And you need this play. And right across the line of scrimmage from you is Jeremiah Trotter. And behind him, there's Brian Dawkins, just looking to take your head off; don't ask me what he did to Ike Hilliard. And just when you're supposed to be making the big play, you'll be thinking, Whoa, Mama! Who am I, and what the fuck am I doing here? And your knees'll start shaking. That can't be good!' "

"Doctor Director?"

"What?"

"Your eye is twitching. You look like you need to lie down, Doc. Uh, there's somethin' running down the side of your mouth there."

"Just give me a second. I got a little carried away. What were we talking about again, Eli?"

"Well, Doctor, I was talkin' about just goin' through my reads . . . and getting the ball to the open man. . . ."

The bus gets its own lane to let us off close to the stadium. It's a big privilege, not having to wade through acres of the Big Blue city encamped outside like the tent city at the foot of the citadel. I keep hoping to find exotic gypsy women banging tambourines and beckoning me into their tents, but all I come across are guys like Sam Fusco, who lives in Summit.

Fusco and pals drive to the games in a creaky junk pile of a bus that looks like it has a million miles on it. He has painted the bus in Giants blue. It is a short bus, the kind they use to take special-needs kids on field trips, so, in a way, it couldn't be more appropriate. On the side, it says, *Touchdown Express.* It comes out after not a lot of talk that Sam, a man in his late sixties, and his pal set fire to a Redskins flag in his backyard once and that other than that he runs an electrical supply store. Sam's résumé—electrical supply store and burned a Redskins flag—immediately impresses me.

For these men, the Jersey men—for everybody—1986 is the year we remember most fondly, the season we cannot help but talk about. Those winter weeks in the Meadowlands. The playoff against Montana and the 49ers. The Giants' Leonard Marshall knocking out Montana . . . L.T.'s interception and touchdown that put the game away 28–0, still in the first half. And the very next week, against the Redskins in the NFC championship game. In the cold and that tornado-like wind . . . booing that Washington creep Dexter Manley off the field and shutting them out 17–0 . . . knowing we were going to the Super Bowl for the first time out in Pasadena to beat the snot out of Denver, and even though Mayor Koch ruled out a ticker tape parade, Chris Mara could lean over and say to Wellington as the paper blizzard of trash blew so hard it looked like confetti, "Fuck Ed Koch, Pop—here's our parade right here."

Back then, a cartographic re-creation of the football world would show the hegemony of the San Francisco 49ers empire. They ruled. They were coached by Bill Walsh, a man so brilliant that his casual expectoration from a moving car window one afternoon on Route 101 happened to land—luckily for the world—on a patch of fertile soil and quickly grew into Silicon Valley.

Walsh's proxy in the huddle was, of course, Joe Montana. Now, as the Manning Bowl kicks off, people may be itching to call Peyton Manning the greatest quarterback ever, but is Eli's big brother as good as Montana? The knock on him is he hasn't won the championship games.

Peyton Manning is looking to separate himself from a long list that includes Elway and Favre and Marino and Stabler and goes back through many, such as Van Brocklin and Sid Luckman and Sammy Baugh.

Here's my method for judging quarterbacks: Who makes you put down your beer? Who makes it so you just stand there and watch, dry-mouthed, while your beer goes flat and unfinished. That would be Johnny Unitas and, currently, the Patriots' Tom Brady, and Montana.

Returning to our cartography of the ancient football world

and the San Francisco empire, how mighty, then, was the one team capable of fighting them off the way the Germanic tribes did the Roman legions? That's how unbreakable the Giants of those years were under their coach, Bill Parcells. In 1984, in his second year, Parcells bugled the Giants into action against the 49ers (who won the Super Bowl that year) and lost. The next year the Giants evened things up, and the year after that beat the 49ers twice and knocked them out of the playoffs en route to their own Super Bowl win. The 49ers beat the Giants in each of the next three seasons.

But then came 1990. The Giants and 49ers were the two best teams in football. The Giants carried a 10–1 record into San Francisco in week 12. In a memorably bruising Monday-night game, the Giants lost 7–3, and the 49ers seemed to have established supremacy.

The 49ers seemed headed toward a record third straight Super Bowl when they faced the Giants for the second time that year, again with home field advantage, this time for the NFC championship. At halftime the score was six apiece. As the final quarter began, the Giants trailed 13–9 after a Montana TD pass.

But Parcells and his Jersey guys were relentless. Leonard Marshall knocked Montana out of the game (and to this day, if you're walking along the street and come within earshot of the man and yell Leonard Marshall loud enough, you can witness the mighty Montana dive headfirst into a trash can for safety).

A fake punt run for thirty yards by one of Parcells's never-ending supply of trusty players, Gary Reasons, set up a fourth field goal.

Still, the defending champs had the ball with 2:36 left and were poised to run out the clock. Montana's sub, Steve Young, handed the ball off to Roger Craig. Erik Howard hit Craig so hard he fumbled. Lawrence Taylor recovered the ball on the Giants' 43. And five plays later, as the gun sounded, Matt Bahr kicked his fifth field goal, and the Giants were headed to the Super Bowl, which they eventually won against Buffalo (on a second straight game-ending field goal, this one missed, by the Bills' Scott Norwood).

When I say that the Giants couldn't have won the Super Bowl against Buffalo if they hadn't beaten San Francisco, I mean more than that. It's what they learned against San Francisco (just as with the 49ers, the Giants had lost to Buffalo in the regular season). That they had it in them to turn the tables in a rematch, with everything on the line. They taught themselves how to be champions.

That's how mentally tough those Jersey teams were. Coached by Parcells, who stood on the sideline making them feel like they'd rather undergo extraordinary rendition than wind up in his office after practice. Who doesn't rue the fact that he isn't coaching the team right now, that he's coaching across the field, coaching the Dallas Cowboys, Tom Landry's old team. "Throw a net over him," a former boss of mine used to say when talking about how seldom real talent happened to cross your path. The Mara family got net-shy when they allowed Vince Lombardi to leave and become the Packers coach and repeated the mistake three decades later, when they let the Tuna swim away.

Of course, Parcells had the best linebacker and the most valuable player in the history of the franchise, Lawrence

Taylor. "The soul of a fighter that rules the body of its possessor," is how the great French fighting general Condé was once described. It fits Taylor in much the same way it fits Shockey now. In the Giants Stadium I imagine over on the Hudson, you'll enter through the grand, marble Lawrence Taylor Lobby.

The play that lives forever in most people's minds about him is the sack that broke the Redskins' Joe Theismann's leg. You can watch LT frantically waving for the stretcher when he sees how gruesome what has befallen Theismann is. Most people see a generosity of spirit in his gesture. But a lip-reader friend of mine claims that this is in fact what LT was yelling: "Hurry up! Get another quarterback in here so I can break that motherfucker's leg, too!"

Parcells treated Taylor one way and his quarterback Phil Simms another, a technique that already sets him apart from Coughlin. Of the two players, Taylor arrived in 1981 sort of *sui generis*. Simms, beginning in 1979, was molded and benched, tossed aside, and hammered back into place. Simms didn't hit his stride until five years in.

And this is what I'm trying to tell Fusco and the rest of his short bus buddies, only they don't want to hear it. They like Simms. And Eli's not Peyton. That's the geometry at work here.

"What about the fourth and seventeen, huh? Remember that play?" Sam keeps telling me, as if I were standing here attacking Simms.

Although Simms had had that brilliant Super Bowl, it remains canon law that his fourth-and-17 sideline pass completion to Bobby Johnson earlier in that glorious season, late in a come-from-behind 22–20 victory at Minnesota, was the finest of the 2,576 he completed in fourteen seasons with the team.

"Huh—what about that? . . . Fourth and fuckin' whatever. Who was that against?"

"Minnesota," six of us say simultaneously, each of us seeing the play again in our minds.

"Yeah, fourth and seventeen . . ."

"All I'm saying is you love Phil Simms so much," I say, "don't you think Eli could be as good as Simms? Would you be happy with that? Eli could be as good as Simms, couldn't he?"

They pause and think about it. But the answer to my mind is unquestionably yes. Eli could be as good as Simms. If he could be as good as Simms, then all we need to turn this team back into those great grinding sons of bitches from the eighties is a coach who will do for Eli what Parcells did for Simms.

"You should come with us sometime," one of the guys on Sam's bus says.

The Manning Bowl settles nothing, as it turns out.

Eli played a good game. He was 20 of 34 for 247 yards and two TD passes, one each to Burress and Shockey. The toss to Burress after an eight-play, 86-yard drive late in the first half to bring the Giants within six points, the 15-yarder bringing them within two, 16–14, to start the second half.

It was stout stuff. Not much difference between younger and older brother. A good enough match so that for weeks afterward people envisioned a rematch, noting with a smile that any rematch for the brothers would, of course, have to come in the Super Bowl, and wouldn't that be something. Eli suffered no decline in estimation after facing his big brother for the first time. If anything, his stock rose. You could picture him standing on the sideline in Miami in February, looking up at the jets streaking over the stadium, getting ready to take Big Blue out onto the Super Bowl field.

But the Giants lost to the Colts. And as well as they played, their many miscues in the game included a fumble, an interception, a rash of foolish penalties. Still, the Giants were just five points down with 1:12 to go when Eli took the offense onto the field at their own 23, the stage set for a defining moment.

Eli threw incomplete, but then passed to Shockey and Toomer and the Giants were in Colts territory with seventeen seconds left. Not much time, but enough for two plays: one shot to get you inside the 30 and then one decent shot at the end zone and for something truly earth-shattering to happen. If Eli could do this, he'd be holding up the severed head of the dragon to a cheering stadium.

I was relishing the prospect, when suddenly a penalty flag was on the field. And the center, Shaun O'Hara, was being called for some weird, technical infraction and the ball was being moved back and ten seconds were automatically being run off the clock so that the Giants were moved back to their own 46 with seven seconds left, and scoring and winning became immediately hopeless.

The stupid penalty at this critical juncture, no less, of their first game, effectively changed everything. At the very least you wanted Eli to be able to say he had one good shot at the end zone to beat his brother, one chance to make one of the plays that live forever. Instead of what it was now, nothing but a Hail Mary desperation pass that fell incomplete as the game ended. The defining test had been taken out of Eli's hands by that one mistake of O'Hara's, which guaranteed the Giants' loss.

That's what I'm stewing about afterward. That maybe Eli could take them all the way. I'm standing at the foot of a ramp leading out from the locker hallways to the parking lots and the practice bubble. After the game, near midnight, rookie defensive end Mathias Kiwanuka stands at the foot of that ramp also. He is with a young woman—friend or family member, I can't tell. But I clock the look on Kiwanuka's face, looking up the incline after his first NFL game. He is taking in everything about the experience, everything about this moment. In the tunnel he looks up and out. His future leads through cheering crowds and out toward a starry night.

What I see in my future is at the very least a heart attack if I miss the bus. You don't want to get stuck in the New Jersey swamp with no way back to the city—ask Jimmy Hoffa. Not that I like waiting on line for the bus home. They load the buses one by one and it can take an hour to get a seat on one. Meanwhile you're ankle-deep, kicking aside discarded cartons, beer cans and shards of glass. Tiptoeing through little puddles of vomit and water and piss and beer and waste.

But before I can head out I glimpse one last player. He walks off the field, his arm swinging, slowly moving, his cleats drumming on the walkway.

It is Peyton Manning. I realize this before I have entirely focused on his face. I realize it from his outline. His silhouette has become that imprinted, almost like Michael Jordan's on the NBA logo. I watch Peyton Manning move by, am in the presence of his ultra–slow motion grandeur as he clomps toward the locker room. This brief sight of him, in full dress, unposed, unwinding postgame, is at once archival and immortal. Peyton Manning. Quarterback.

After the game, the parking lot is depressing. It empties quickly. It is littered with discarded trash and spilled-out drinks. The stadium is stripped of the interest so much focused attention has lent it. It's even worse, of course, when the home team has lost.

It is a somber ride home. Sure, it was close and wouldn't it be something if the two—teams and brothers—met again in the Super Bowl. But it was just the first game of the season and nothing was settled.

I can't help feeling, however, that something has been settled. And that there will be more stadium lots and bus rides like tonight and not many merry last calls at P. J. Clarke's for me before I finally get home to my apartment. Peyton Manning, it strikes me, has taken all the grown-up out of the house with him.

The bus crawls through bumper-to-bumper traffic back toward the city and finally from the Weehawken heights I see the towers of Manhattan. The lights are muted the way they get late on a Sunday night when something still has finally taken hold of the city before the big town shakes it off and starts up again.

I envision, there, on the far side of the river, the Mara stadium I want to see built, its Giants blue lights glinting off the black water. The field lights burst upward, powdering the sky. But darkness rushes at my head as we duck into the tunnel and a voice suddenly pops into my brain. It is my big brother. And he has two words for Eli and me:

"Think fast," he shouts.

Chapter 5

1-800-BITE-ME

So my wife and I got a new bed. A California King. This sounds great rolling off the tongue—California King; it makes you feel like you own Seabiscuit, doesn't it?—but try finding your wife in it. She's over there somewhere, barely visible on the other side, a bulge in the horizon line, basically, in some way not even in the same room. There ought to be a signpost in the middle of my bed, one of those wooden arrows that reads: *Pussy Five Miles.*

Supposedly it's this Restless Leg Syndrome again. Staying outside twitching distance has made my wife's life better. But she seems all too content to sleep without me when I'm gone on one of my innumerable trips across the country to watch the Giants. Back and forth to New York. I just returned from Seattle. She used to be a nervous wreck when my warm body wasn't around.

"This is so much better," my wife says, patting all the space around her and settling in to watch a movie in our new California King. No movie can be too grim for her. All sorts of children have to be orphaned and many women widowed and buckets of bone marrow matched. The kind of movie that just makes me want to belch like a sea lion.

"There's nothing good on," she says. She picks up a book to read. She's getting a graduate degree and has been reading lots of Chekhov stories lately, along with Tolstoy and Balzac. She's got *The Golden Bowl* by Henry James in her hands now, and she's explaining the lapidary perfection in the story of poor Charlotte and the Italian prince Amerigo, in love but with no fortune, admiring that bowl with a crack in a London curio shop, and how her rich friend Maggie had married the Prince instead and how Maggie had encouraged Charlotte's marriage to Maggie's father and how this arrangement kept everything morally dubious but satisfying to all concerned. Maggie could maintain her unhealthy, close relationship with her father and Charlotte and the Prince could continue their love affair.

"But then, one day," my wife says, "there's a knock on the door and it's a delivery for Maggie from that shop in London. And the guy who's delivering the Golden Bowl sees a picture of Charlotte in Amerigo's house. And he tells Maggie he's seen the two of them together in his shop, admiring this very golden bowl. And Maggie realizes she's been betrayed. By the Golden Bowl. It's an amazing moment that Henry James has taken. . . . four hundred pages to set up. Are you listening?"

"Yeah," I say a little too weakly.

"What?"

"I think John Mara wants to punch me in the nose."

"Who?"

"John Mara."

"Who's he again?"

"One of the owners."

"Of who, the Giants?"

"Yeah."

"He wants to punch you in the nose?"

"Probably."

"That's what you're lying here thinking about? While I'm trying to tell you about the Golden Bowl?"

"Yeah."

"I'm talking about Henry James and you're obsessing about John Mara?"

It was halftime of the Seattle game, I tell her. She puts down the book and tries to pay attention, so I spell it out: How the Seahawks and their puffy, hyphen-mouthed coach, Mike Holmgren, went to the Super Bowl last year, but if you look at how the Giants played them, you were not convinced Seattle was better. We only lost because of three missed field goals and so many mistakes, particularly by left tackle Luke Pettigout, that he called himself "an embarrassment to my family." (Which made me wonder, if four illegal procedure calls qualified you as an embarrassment to your family, what did my life make me?)

At any rate, we'd awaited a rematch for ten months. This was a significant game—far more than the ballyhooed opener, the Manning Bowl, and in a way more important than the Eagles game they'd played in week two, which they'd won. The Giants had talked of a Super Bowl all summer—well, now they got the chance to play one of the teams from the previous year's match-up.

But the rematch during the last week of September was a catastrophe. The score was 28–0 at the end of the first quarter. The Giants kicker, Jay Feeley, who missed three kicks that would have beaten the Seahawks in last year's game, finally made one, ten months and twenty-nine minutes too late, nailing it just before halftime to make the score 35–3.

At the interval the media grabbed foil-wrapped hot dogs and sodas and chips. Behind the press-row arcade in Seattle there's a narrow space with several tables and chairs along the wall. There are TV monitors on which the writers can watch halftime reports and other games in progress. Grabbing a hot dog and some chips, I slumped to a place at one of the tables.

Directly across from me, facing away and sipping a soda, John Mara sat brooding by himself. Coming toward us was former Giants head coach Dan Reeves, who was headed for one or another broadcast booth along electronic media row. Reeves, passing his old acquaintance, naturally thought to exchange a greeting with John. He slowed, taking John in, but before speaking, caught a full-on glance at John's face, which, though I couldn't directly see it, clearly wore a "Not welcome" expression. And so Reeves simply smiled, patted John's arm twice and then, with a benign and not unsympathetic chuckle at the situation, kept walking. There was nothing to say.

Dan's chuckle seemed to find a wry, worldly amusement in John's plight. Dan had been with the team for four years as head coach in the mid-'90s, and when the Giants went into the tank, which was pretty much every year after his first— those were the Dave Brown years, after all—at least he had white-haired, rosary-rubbing Wellington Mara to console him. John didn't. It was 35–3, and Reeves seemed to be saying, "It's your team now, kid, and ain't you havin' fun?"

That's when my cell phone rang. It was my thirteen-year-old daughter back home. She, too, had just seen the first half. She doesn't always watch the games, but she had taken an interest and wanted to offer her halftime report, only it was different from Howie and Jimmy and Terry's frat boy chortle-and-noogie routine.

She was sobbing hysterically. Here's how 35–3 translated to her: The Giants are lousy. They are so lousy your book will get canceled. No book, no money.

"Am I going to have to leave school?" she wailed over the phone as I sat in the Seattle press box trying to deal with the 35–3 score. She thought her life was over.

"What?"

"Please don't make me leave school, Daddy."

"Nobody's doing that."

"The Giants stink, Dad. Are we gonna lose our house, Dad?"

"Don't be ridiculous, sweetie."

"You promise?"

"Of course not," I said. "The Giants are going to be fine. Calm down."

"We won't be poor?" she said, sniffling. "You promise?"

"I'm positive."

"They could still win?"

Here is where you have the option of letting either the truth or your daughter slip from your arms. I held on to my daughter and lied.

"Of course they can still win. I'm sure they can."

"You think so?"

"Sure I do, so don't worry," I said.

I hung up.

The fuck the Giants are going to win, I thought. The announcers are saying the team will have to make some half-time adjustments.

But what I'm afraid they're really doing is exactly what my daughter's doing—sobbing hysterically. There's probably a big pile of rapidly emptied Kleenex boxes in the middle of their locker room.

Man alive! 35–3?

I'm practically sobbing myself.

"What're you going to do?" I said loud enough for John Mara's ears. "Imagine a kid getting that riled up about a game. They take it so hard, y'know?"

John Mara appeared not to hear me. Although I did discern what could be construed as a twitch (is it possible that John Mara is a fellow RLS sufferer?).

"I mean, they go crazy, they have no perspective. Like it was life or death," I went on. "But you and I know it's more important than that, eh?" I chortled nervously, hoping to penetrate the force field of doom around Mara. But the more I projected my voice the more fatuous I sounded. I told myself my purpose was to elicit from him something philosophical, some family wisdom gleaned over eight decades of winning and losing, but he didn't respond and my words began clanging in my ears. "It can't help but get to you, doesn't it? I mean, it's such a downer, what do *you* do? A score like 35–3? Man alive!"

John Mara finally turned. His eyes bored in on me and narrowed into dull gray slugs of loathing.

After regarding me venomously, John stiffly returned to what he was watching on the TV for a few moments so he wouldn't appear impolite when he got up to leave the vicinity. When he did finally go, I thought I detected the word "numb-nuts" under his breath.

As I watched him leave I felt a stinging redness flash across my face, with pins and needles. It felt as if I had just been socked in the nose. I'd asked for it. Talk about inappropriate stupidity when the right thing to do was, as Dan Reeves saw, or anyone with a brain would have known, to shut the fuck up.

Was that my daughter sniffling or me? She had sought reassurance from me. I had just sought it from John Mara. I was not only now thinking like a thirteen-year-old, I was behaving like a thirteen-year-old.

All these travails I recount to my wife, who appears to be inching farther and farther away from me across the arid wastes of our California King.

"Somehow," my wife says after listening to my story, "I doubt that wherever he is, John What's-His-Name is spending a second thinking about you."

She picks up *The Golden Bowl* as if she needs her mind re-intellectualized as quickly as possible, flexes the book's spine with a sharp, proprietary crack, adjusts the pillows propping her back with a few slaps and daintily draws down across her tongue the tip of her right forefinger, moistening it so she can most efficiently whip-turn the novel's page and continue reading. All of which makes it crystal-clear to me that from now on whatever pleasure and stimulation my wife gets out of great literature and, perhaps, great art and music too, there is no way she will share it with me.

Like the thirteen-year-old I was aping, I feel put down and get surly. I need support for this vertiginous descent back into the depths of time, not contempt. And if I am regressing into adolescence, it might be prudent to ponder, before I regress any further and while I still maintain reasonably mature judgment, what we *would* do if, as my daughter seemed to fear with increasingly good reason, they did cancel my book because the Giants were so bad. And we did go broke. And did get thrown out of the house.

Could the three of us live in the Prius?

That is what I need to be thinking about anyway, and so does my wife, and not whether the ending of *The Golden Bowl* left Prince Amerigo and Charlotte and Maggie and the rest of human civilization better or worse off. We need to be thinking about whether the New York Giants are going to leave us better or worse off.

I realize I have reached the point where I need what the players get in the NFL, a "cooling-off period." To get over the games. I probably need a really long one, much longer than the players get, which is about a dozen minutes. I don't know how Tiki does it.

"The hardest part about the games really is taking your shirt off afterward," Tiki told me. "It's so hard. You're so tired. Your shoulders or something may hurt. And those pads and jerseys are so tight, it's like you really have to have someone pull it off of you. You take your pads off, you kind of just chill for two minutes and the coach brings you up, gives you a speech, you say the Lord's Prayer. Then you have probably ten minutes to kind of sit down. And then I get in the shower, talk to the other guys in the shower, talk about the game, whatever, and then usually by that time, you're calm, you're together. I get dressed and then I kind of turn around and take the questions."

By the time the media gets to the players you can hear the hiss from the showers, the slap of bare feet on tile and the low hum of the men immersing their bruises in the spatter and consolatory steam. The players emerge in towels, go to their lockers. They turn their backs to the room to dress—a nod to propriety for the sake of the female reporters there—give themselves a quick pat-down and pull on their pants. By then they have steadied themselves with some anodyne version of "We've got to play better next week," or "Our backs are up against the wall." But after the Seattle game, there wasn't enough hot water in all the locker rooms of Christendom to help the Giants cool down. If the sixty minutes of football I'd just watched had been an episode of a one-hour TV series, I'd have said cancel the show.

In the locker room after the Seattle game, Jeremy Shockey sat down in front of his locker, legs splayed in royal disregard for decorum, and said, "We were outplayed and outcoached— you can write that down."

Most of the other players had dressed and yanked out the pull-handles of their carry-on suitcases and rolled outside for a cheap box meal before boarding the bus. Shockey didn't have an appetite. He had some things to get off his chest. So much so that he stepped into a media scrum that had surrounded offensive tackle Luke Pettitgout, who was being interviewed next to him.

Shockey slowly pulled on a gray-blue pair of sweats, unable to conceal a scornful laugh when he heard that minutes earlier, down the hall at the podium, coach Tom Coughlin had been blaming the defeat on a "loss of composure."

"Composure" is not high on the list of attributes Jeremy Shockey models. Did you see him on the last play of the hopeless Seattle game, catching a pass, purposely not going out of bounds, purposely not avoiding a hit he could have avoided and that, surely, no weary Seahawk really wanted to risk delivering? Instead, Shockey turned back in, lowered his head and plowed into two tacklers, ending the game seconds after the clock had already run out, but getting one last lick in, and then tapping his opponents' helmets respectfully when he unpiled.

Shockey!

Football doesn't have 162 games. Only 16 battles decide this war to see who'll make the playoffs. The brutality is endless, the season fleeting, and the fortunes of every team and every player are suspended between success and failure on each snap across the razor's edge that is the hash mark. It may be only the third game of the season, and two losses to two of the four best teams in the league need not leave the Giants feeling downcast, but it seemed as if something not very salutary had resurfaced, or at the very least revealed itself to be there just under the surface, should things remain as frustrating as they became that afternoon in Seattle.

There have been a couple books out lately, and one pointy-headed piece I read in the *New Yorker*, to the effect that football is becoming more and more like the computer games it inspired. It has become so overprogrammed it is reducible to pixels.

But you cannot be the human equivalent of a search engine hoping to find a 290-pound sixth-grader who will turn into a left tackle someday. Why? For one thing, catastrophic injury is ever present. Every play could be your last. There are no more darkly empty words among so many platitudes cast at the best players than these: for many years to come.

There is, effectively, no reliable future in the NFL. Contracts are not guaranteed. But let's proceed in the study of player husbandry, searching for the perfectly bred lineman. I have two words for you: Tony Mandarich (picked No. 1 by Green Bay in 1998). You know: bench-presses 900 pounds, vertical leap of 30 feet, 26-inch waist, 27-inch biceps, runs the 40 in 3.9. You hear about a few of him every year. One of dozens of guys who work their way out of Michelangelo's workshop onto the cover of *Sports Illustrated* and wind up playing in the league for, oh, about sixteen seconds. Ultimately, success isn't about anything you measure at a Combine workout.

The Giants' linebacker Antonio Pierce came out of Arizona as an undrafted free agent. Unfucking drafted. Of the 704 players in the starting offensive and defensive lineups on opening day '06, only a handful, including Pierce, had been, in effect, told by the experts not to bother. With that chip soldered onto his shoulder, Pierce has concocted his own sort of tontine, an abstruse compact by which members agree that whoever is the last alive will receive the others' money. In Pierce's personally customized version, he keeps track of the thirty college linebackers who were drafted in the class of 2001—in other words, all those who were adjudged by stopwatches and scales and whatever else scouts can measure to be better than Pierce—and feels himself enriched as he gets closer and closer to being the last to survive in the league. As the season begins, only thirteen are left. So Pierce, more than most, understands the basics: Once they flip the coin, the draft, the general manager, the Combine in February mean shit. Once they flip the coin it is only about effort and attention to detail.

The sixty or seventy-plus plays a game compose a narrative, each possession a paragraph, each play a sentence with a subject and a predicate. An action, or inquiry, if you will, and a response. What you weigh and how fast you run don't mean or say anything, don't compose what every team needs, a story. And what the Giants, collectively, incontrovertibly, communicated against Seattle was incoherence.

Which brings us back to the halftime score in Seattle: 35–3.

"They were in defenses that we didn't know they were going to be in," Shockey said after the Seahawks debacle, sallying forth into areas he knew were better left alone, the way he just had on the football field, game over but plowing in head-first, looking to deliver a lick. "They did different things that we hadn't seen [in practice]. You can make adjustments all you want, but when they switch things up we can't do anything."

Shockey vowed, "I'm not going to shit myself again," by being vocally critical of the coaches as he had been way back in training camp. But by this time, Giants staff were wearing alarmed expressions and began insisting that Shockey would miss the bus if he didn't finish getting dressed and grab a meal.

Shockey pulled on a way-too-tight T-shirt that read, *How's My Driving? Call 1-800-Bite Me*, and said, sarcastically, "I'll probably get fined for wearing this," before joining his less vocally disgruntled teammates.

The New York Giants were penned into a small roped-off area about twelve feet square. A bunch of cheap portable picnic tables were squeezed inside it. Before catching the plane, the Giants, ties barely knotted and heads barely dried, jammed into that small space and shoveled down some grub. Right there. In the corridor, in the concrete catacomb. Above them and around them, deliriously happy Seattle fans ran up and down the ramps cheering. Curious passersby peered at the large men made to feel small, eating the box suppers in the dusty corner beneath the pounding droves on the stadium stairway.

I felt my molars involuntarily tap, ready to grind.

Just as I do tonight, here in my California King, feeling like I've been socked in the nose.

Chapter 6

Once a Giant, Always a Giant

No sooner had the football Giants of 1956 untied their sneakers in the locker room after their championship victory than they became the template for what the Buffalo Bills turned into decades later—a great team that reached the finals and lost. Every time. In '58, '59, '61, and '62.

Each loss felt as if it was being pounded against my pre-adolescent heart by that sweaty-armed man who blasted the metal hammer at the end of each *Dragnet* episode. A Mark VII Production. I learned at a young age right there in my very own den that there were some mortal hurts that my father was helpless to protect me from. And that he, therefore, was mortal too.

Finally, in 1963, the Giants got to play for the title against a team that wasn't as clearly great as either Unitas's Colts (in

Quarterback Y. A. Tittle and the Giants lost the 1963 championship game to the Bears, 14–10, after the Bears nearly broke Tittle's leg. Not that I'm bitter. NEIL LEIFER

'58 and '59) or (in '61 and '62) Lombardi's Green Bay Packers. This nourished hope that in a new, third opponent—the Chicago Bears—the cure for the plague of winter heartsickness might be at hand.

The Giants may not have been a better team than the Colts or the Packers, but they were better than the Chicago Bears in 1963. New York averaged something like 32 points a game. And there was one great advantage. At quarterback they had Y. A. Tittle, who passed the ball as if he were young, although, confoundingly to me, he was as bald as an old man. Chicago had some guy named Billy Wade, who'd been in the league for years without making the name for himself Y. A. had since starting out with the 49ers.

The Giants began the title game so well—with a great touchdown strike to Frank Gifford—that as he trotted off the field following the score, Gifford assured his coach, Allie Sherman, "Coach, we're gonna beat the shit out of these guys."

Chicago's only hope was to knock Tittle out of the game. So that's basically what they did. One of the Bears' linebackers, Larry Morris, slammed low into Tittle's left leg as he planted and threw a pass in the second quarter (cf. *Andre Waters v. Phil Simms*). His knee shredded, Tittle could barely stand the rest of the game, had to take two shots of Novocain and be taped up at halftime.

In the cheapest sports victory in history, the Bears won the 1963 title at Soldier Field, 14–10.

A year and a half later, in July, I had a chance to win that title back for the Giants. I was in Evanston, studying journalism for a month at Northwestern, a J-school boot camp for teenagers with a faculty of journalists and nonfiction writers. We were called "cherubs."

One day we filed into an auditorium where we were told we would have an exercise in writing a news story based on a press conference. We were going to interview a special guest.

There were three or four dozen of us cherub journalists seated (including Frank Rich, who's done pretty well in journalism since), but I believe I was the only one who instantly recognized the special guest we were being introduced to.

He was Billy Wade. The quarterback of the Chicago Bears, who'd beaten the Giants eighteen months earlier. Northwestern was, after all, not far from the Bears' summer training camp.

Wade looked like a man who preferred injecting himself with flesh-eating bacteria to standing in front of an audience of fifteen- and sixteen-year-olds, none of whom, it was quickly apparent, knew anything about him or much about football, and certainly not that he was what I knew him to be—the fraudulent holder of the NFL's championship title.

The instructors had spent weeks drumming into us the imperatives of fact and objectivity. I believed in them.

But I also believed in the New York Giants. And I remained sufficiently obsessed to be well aware of what was going on at football training camps that summer.

The other cherubs began questioning Wade ultra-earnestly. "What university did you attend, Mr. Wade?"

"*Vanderbilt.*"

"Where is that located, sir?"

"*Nashville, Tennessee.*"

"Two n's and two s's?"

"*That's right.*"

"Is training camp fun like other camps? Is there canoeing?"

"*No, no canoeing.*"

Meanwhile, I composed a better question. My question went something like this:

"Mr. Wade, the man who coaches your defense, Mr. George Allen, is reportedly feuding with head coach Halas. There are rumors George Allen wants a head coaching job somewhere else and Halas is standing in his way. Do you think that Coach Allen deserves all the credit he claims or is he someone who bends the rules for his own good? Isn't he a cheater?"

I wasn't sure what Billy Wade would say, but I realized, as I formulated the question and waited to ask it with my heart thumping nervously, that I wasn't interested in his answer. I already knew the answer to the question. Billy Wade, quarterback of the 1963 NFL champion Chicago Bears, would hear my question in that lecture hall at Northwestern and he would say something like this:

"Our team has only one head coach—George Halas. Not George Allen. And so I'd have to answer yes, that George Allen is a little sneaky . . . he does bend the rules. You know, standing here in front of young people like you . . . it makes me feel like it's important to know right from wrong. . . ."

At this point Wade's voice catches. He's mentioned the array of young faces before him and now takes a longer look, all his crew-cut toughness disarmed by our massed innocence.

"In fact, I prob'ly shouldn't be mentioning this. But the season before last, that championship we won . . . the one Coach Allen takes all the credit for . . . he told his defense to go out there and injure Y. A. Tittle. What's your name, son?" he asks, looking out into the audience.

I clear my throat.

"Roger," I say.

"Well, Rog," he says, "I'm actually glad you've asked me that question. Because now I've got a chance to get something off my chest, something that's been weighing on me a long time. It's about Coach Allen. He told our defense our only hope was to make it so Y. A. couldn't be his normal self in that game. To knock him out or cripple him if we could. He told us to play dirty. That it would be okay. It'd just be a fifteen-yard penalty but if we hurt Tittle we could win. And to back it up, he offered a free steak dinner to whichever of his players hurt Tittle so the Giants couldn't win the game. I've felt a little guilty about that for the longest time."

A smile of relief gets the better of Wade here. He turns and waves out the door of the lecture hall, and says:

"You know, it so happens I have the 1963 championship trophy outside in the parking lot in the backseat of my car. We each get turns holding on to it for a day. But hearing the question this young man asked, and having a chance to think it over, I don't believe it belongs to us. I think it belongs to the Giants. I know I'm going to get in trouble for saying this, but we did cheat in the championship game. The Giants were a better team. And I think it's time everyone admitted it. I'm sure some people in Chicago will hate me, but it's the right thing, so I'm going to go out to my car and get that NFL trophy and hand it to this young man so he can take it personally to the Mara family, the fine family who really deserve this trophy. If there's some kind of F.B.I. investigation about this, I don't care, let the chips fall where they may. From now on I won't cheat anyone ever again."

I was still imagining myself standing there, holding the NFL championship trophy that Billy Wade put in my hands for delivery to the Maras and contemplating how I was going to get to the airport in Chicago to take the trophy back and whether I had enough for the cab fare and just what a scoop this was, the kind of scoop that would make Walter Cronkite, the kind of scoop that would land me an ace job with a great newspaper like the *New York Times*, when I heard one of the instructors calling my name and telling me it was my chance to ask Mr. Wade a question.

I couldn't yank my tongue off the roof of my mouth. It was Velcro-d.

"Whu—whadyathinka Gracie Allen?" I stammered out.

I heard laughter.

"I'm not sure what you mean, son."

"Sorry. I meant George Allen."

"He's defense, I'm offense, so we don't work together a whole lot."

The boy who fumbled that question clearly wasn't destined to grow up and become one of the daily-beat reporters who cover the Giants. Ralph Vacchiano of the *News*. Paul Schwartz of the *Post*. John Branch of the *Times*. John Altavilla of the *Hartford Courant*. The *Star-Ledger*'s Mike Garafalo.

The people who cover the Giants don't have it easy. Put yourself in their shoes for a second and think of how much the writers have lost in the last couple years, how seriously degraded their fun has gotten. They had Coach Fassel holding pizza-and-film parties at night, a guy who you could could pop in and schmooze with. In place of him there's Tom

"There's Hitler and Then Me" Coughlin. And now they've lost Accorsi, a most simpatico GM, a onetime sportswriter himself and an engaging raconteur.

The sportswriters stay in dives on the road. And think of where the sportswriters work when they're not in the luxurious press box. The beat guys have a dinky dungeon room in the bowels of the Meadowlands.

At training camp in Albany, the press room faced an interior courtyard, on the opposite side of which was the large dining hall where everyone—players, coaches and media—ate at staggered times. The writers weren't allowed to walk across the courtyard into the dining hall—about thirty feet. Nor were they supposed to walk through the adjacent PR office to get to the dining hall. The writers had to exit the press room into the courtyard, go up a flight of stairs, walk about two hundred yards away from the cafeteria, descend another flight of stairs, then walk back around the building to the front of the cafeteria to eat. At least ten times the distance and trouble it needed to be.

The exercise wasn't the problem. The problem was the cinderblock that was the only way of keeping open the heavy door to the inner courtyard so the writers could go in and out. Every few seconds, the door swung shut and you'd hear:

CONGHHH!!!

You know what that sounds like at unpredictable—*CONGHHH!!!*

—intervals?

It was a sonic torture chamber, it seemed to me, for anyone trying to make a deadline. It amazed me that the beat writers could keep their wits about them. Not to mention churn out the requisite two thousand words a day. But these are tougher people than me. They can sit in the press box and not cheer.

I'm finding that harder and harder. Post-Seattle, the Giants have turned things around and begun rampaging across the Steppes. Spreading the Word to the sea. Supposedly, it was the bye week, that game hiatus each team gets during the season. The players got together the first week of October, snapped a few jockstraps and emerged with new resolve. A few days ago, on Monday night, October 23, the Giants won in Dallas.

At the end of the first half, with the Cowboys driving for a score, Drew Bledsoe improbably tossed an interception at the goal line. The throw was supposed to go to the right. To Terrell Owens, the great receiver you can't help thinking would have lasted about one quarter on Johnny Unitas's team before Johnny figured out an ingenious way to have him carried off the field on two stretchers. Bledsoe's reaction was to throw away from Owens, to the other side, where it was intercepted. Parcells, his mouth a puckered sphincter, yanked Bledsoe in favor of a kid named Tony Romo, aptly named as if for some soda jerk in a Warners melodrama of the '30s, who throws aside his apron and steps out from behind the counter to lead his team to victory. Not on this night, though, even if he did seem to spark the team and is a favorite of the fans.

Seeing his coronation as the new Cowboy quarterback, you can't help praying to the heavens that somewhere along the line, when he's got his team on the verge of something great, Tony Romo's pluck will run out, and in a way so cruel only Satan could think it up. (This is, in fact, the tithe-worthy miracle that happens in a playoff late in the year against Seattle, where Romo botches a simple field-goal hold, turning a sure victory into an improbable, cataclysmic failure, calling to mind the image of that croc hunter, Steve Irwin, swimming playfully behind a stingray, suddenly pulling a barb from his chest and floating away, like the Cowboys, dead.).

But let's not forget Bledsoe's unfortunate fate. Drafted as the No. 1 overall pick by Parcells in New England. Brought by Parcells to save things in Dallas. And, in the last act, benched by Parcells in public view, at halftime on national TV. The last pass of his career an interception.

Merciless world. Merciless life. Merciless league. The bulk of Giants Stadium, looming over the swamp reeds, is a boneyard as much as a playing field. Your chances of staying in the cast of characters on the field is about as good as if you were an actor in a mayhem-filled, one-hour soap opera, and maybe worse. Poison! Car crash! Fell off a cliff! Half the players on the field won't be in this same position next year. LeVar Arrington—No. 1 overall pick in the draft. Pettigout—the team's top pick in 1999. Released.

Think, for example, of the playoff game against Carolina in '05, the final seconds of an NFL life belonging to Terrell Buckley. Buckley, drafted out of Florida State in 1992, was one of the great defensive backs in NFL history. One of only seventeen players with at least fifty career interceptions. Yet there he was, in the winter of 2005 in the most important game of the season, having not played in a solid year since being let go by the Jets. The Giants, in crisis mode, in their desperate injury triage by season's end, picked up Buckley at age thirty-four for their first playoff game. On the field that day, Buckley was the only player on the Giants to own a Super Bowl ring (when he played for New England). But he was also five years past his prime and two seconds late in getting over to cover wideout Steve Smith on a Carolina touchdown pass to the post.

So a future Hall of Famer says good-bye, getting beat like a drum in the last moments of a life ten thousand plays long. A body bag burned on a fire. A man in the middle of the tracks.

Tiki does not want to let that happen to him. Word has gotten out in mid-October that this season will be his last. That he is calling it quits. Fans and sportswriters have felt betrayed and been angry. Barber, who has been the face of the team, its emblem, stands accused of being a distraction, a problem, a torpedo hole beneath the waterline.

I'm not surprised by Barber's news. The first day at summer training camp, Barber showed up in a dandyish tattersall vest and matching cap—so "finished," so chosen—and made a point of how he was not sure he'd play through the end of his contract, which had two more years to run. Your last day isn't the thing to be talking about on your first day, I had thought, and I took it as a clear hint of something I'd suspected for a while.

Months earlier, at P. J.'s in the spring of '06, Barber had talked about how drained he felt following a season marked by the deaths of the team's two owners. Tiki lives on the East Side but wasn't familiar with the history of the saloon and its football ghosts. And at P. J.'s, the ghosts teased from Tiki the truth about how much the '05 season had meant. He was talking to all of them. To Jack Mara and Ken Strong. To Rosey Brown and Sam Huff. To L. T. To Big Red. To Joe Morris and Ron Johnson and Del Shofner. To Ward Cuff and Bill Swiacki and Eddie Price. To Ray Flaherty and Ed Danowski, Harry Newman and Mel Hein and Arnie Weinmeister. And to Steve Owen. They were all there, listening.

"Given what we went through, having to adapt to the loss of our two owners . . . that was a historic season for us," he said over lunch. "And not because of the wins and losses, but because of what we lost. So to me, losing to Carolina in the playoffs was not just another loss. It was something much deeper, you know? And it was disappointment, anger, it was all these different emotions bottled up in one, in me, because I have an understanding what this organization is. We had the opportunity to do something, you know, and we'll never have that opportunity again. Yeah, we may win a Super Bowl in 2006, but we won't have the opportunity to do it in a year that was so historic for a lot of reasons.

"So, after the season ended, I took about two weeks off and started working out again. One because I hated thinking about the playoff loss, so I wanted to start thinking about next season, 2006. And the problem is for me now at age thirty—I'll be thirty-one next month—it's daunting to think about what it's going to take to meet my own physical, mental commitment to start working out, pushing myself, going through mini-camp, going through training camp, going through a whole regular season, and get back to that point. It's daunting to think about it. The mental is daunting. To make yourself want to do it again."

For Tiki, then, his most significant season, 2005, was gone irretrievably. Even a potential Super Bowl ring offered insufficient recompense. And when you're not playing for the title, there is really nothing left except joy and money, and Tiki doesn't need the latter.

What seems to turn disappointment into anger among some outsiders in the wake of the news that this is Tiki's last season is that it is self-scheduled. He wants to leave on his own terms. This seems to partake of blasphemy, the sort that wrinkles foreheads and tightens workingmen's callused grips around beer mug handles down at the Blarney Stone.

Tiki wants to remain intact. And this infuriates people who wish two things in life: achieving recognition or "fame" and remaining intact. Not everyone can be famous or recognized for their quality—but of one thing all mankind, high and low, can rest assured: Despite what you might wish, nobody, goddammit, nobody gets to leave here intact. You do not get to leave on your terms.

No, Tiki, you'll beg and cry like the rest of us. You'll long and self-recriminate and thrash in bed at night. Maybe you'll even be the last one to learn about it, the way the rest of us do. Maybe you won't get told face-to-face, man to man. Maybe you won't even get a call. That's the way it works for the rest of us. Nobody gets out of here intact. Especially in football. Football and intact cannot coexist. Ask Terrell Buckley. Ask LeVar Arrington. Ask Luke Pettigout. Ask Chad Morton. Ask Carlos Emmons. Ask Drew Bledsoe.

No sooner has the *Times* broken the retirement news than Tiki has to weather a storm of criticism, and he has an uncharacteristic verbal tussle with *Daily News* columnist Gary Meyers after calling him, as well as ESPN commentators Tom Jackson and Michael Irvin, idiots for slamming the timing of his retirement announcement.

"I think everyone in this locker room, including myself, we all realize my personal decision has no effect on the 2006 football season," Tiki says in response. "It has a great effect on 2007, but no effect on this season. My role as a leader on this team extends from encouraging other players, getting [backup running back] Brandon Jacobs ready, to playing with the same passion and excitement and courage that I always do, and that's what I've done so far. So anybody who thinks otherwise is not paying attention to what's going on."

Actually, Tiki has to weather more than reporters and disillusioned fans in the Dallas game. On a short-yardage play, going over the middle, Tiki takes a handoff and is hit by the Cowboys' DeMarcus Ware, a lethal linebacker. Ware, it appears to me, isn't even going for the tackle or the ball; he is, in fact, even if only by happenstance, an agent of the gods, of what the ancients might call the *logos* or the indifferent genius of the world.

Ware crashes like a Jovian thunderbolt straight into Tiki's jawbone, the sort of hit, helmet to helmet, that gets people fined and flags thrown.

In midair, having already left his feet, Tiki is knocked out. That's the way it looks to me. You can see his eyelids flutter. He is comatose in the air. The ball drops from his grasp and fumbles out onto the field and Tiki falls back to the ground limply and onto his back, blacked out. He lies there for a moment and to me he looks dead, maybe. It is a brush with death.

Don't think it isn't.

Most players would have come out for the rest of the game. But Tiki couldn't. After all, it had just been announced that this was to be his last season, and even if his head had been separated from his shoulders and had gone rolling along the sideline, coming to a stop beneath Tom Coughlin, had Tiki sat out the rest of the game people would have called him a slacker, someone biding time until retirement and not giving his all. The team *politeia* is built on trust.

And so, in an unremarked act of fortitude that would have made Terry Molloy proud, Tiki had to get to his feet. Had to blink himself back to consciousness and wobble back to work. For trust's sake. Okay, maybe it wasn't like the end of *On the Waterfront*. But he knew, and accepted willingly, that his every play would be seen as a test of whether he was a quitter. This is a worthy standard by which a man should be judged, let alone a pro football player. Let's not even try to guess what percentage of men rise to that standard.

Or fail to meet it. That's the real contact sport. The real game film. Viewed on the ceiling at 3 A.M. Staring from the pillow. Was I a chickenshit today . . . did I run out of bounds?

The early part of the season was the most challenging, and here they are, 4–2, two games over .500. They have beaten Dallas in Dallas. They have beaten Philadelphia in Philadelphia, thanks to a raging fourth-quarter comeback led by young Manning, who audibled a 31-yard touchdown pass in OT to Burress. And who had gotten them into position to kick the tying field goal in regulation with an unflinching 22-yard completion to Tim Carter that he nothing less than expertly lofted over the middle while being dragged to his knees by the Eagles' Darren Howard. It was among his five best passes of the season. Eli was showing a little of a great quarterback's larcenous spirit. A great quarterback has to love breaking people's hearts. Maybe Eli was learning to like the taste of blood.

Not even halfway into the season—and despite the loss to Seattle and the loss to the Colts—the Giants own an almost insurmountable lead within their own division. They merely need to beat either the Eagles or the Cowboys in return engagements at the Meadowlands, something no team with a real claim to merit would be unable to do.

Returning home to face Tampa after Dallas figures to be relatively easy. Especially because the Bucs don't have their regular quarterback, Chris Simms, son of the Giants' former great, Phil. Chris wouldn't be playing because of an equipment shortage—he didn't have his spleen. It had been knocked out in a game the previous week.

On top of what figured to be an easy win the last Sunday in October, pushing the record to 5–2, there was also a special halftime celebration—it was old-timers day. I'd been awaiting this since the first day of training camp in July when I introduced myself to the Giants' VP of communications, the loyal Pat Hanlon, my first or second question being, what did the Giants intend doing to celebrate the fiftieth anniversary of their 1956 title team.

The '56 team was really the first one that brought the league to life, that defined a cast of resourceful winning characters who'd won over Madison Avenue pretty much the way Davy Crockett had. It was this team, the '56 Giants, that brought attention to the league two years before the fabled sudden-death loss against the Colts. The '56 team built the league. The team I'd been listening to way back when in my den. The team that whipped Chicago, 47–7.

Hanlon just looked at me. My breath didn't smell of alcohol, but he wasn't yet ready to rule out the possibility that I was drunk. It wasn't the first time someone had regarded me as if I were being overenthusiastic.

"It's the fiftieth anniversary, you know. Of course you know, why am I telling you? You know better than me. I mean, the '56 team . . . it's like when President Reagan went to Normandy forty years after D-day, they had a big celebration, they made speeches." I sort of drew myself up into presidential bearing and declaimed:

" 'These are the boys of Pointe du Hoc. These are the men who took the cliffs. These are the champions who helped free a continent.' "

"We'll have sump'n," Hanlon said. "Mr. Mara'd usually take 'em out to dinner. He's not around this year, so my guess is John'll do it."

"Of course," I said, and I told him how I supposed it would be, explaining that, as a television producer, I could see taking this idea, packaging it, bringing all the elements together. There'd have to be the arrival, of course. A procession of limousines pulling up to Gallagher's Steak House maybe. Or, of course, P. J. Clarke's. Red-carpet interviews. Cameras at the dinner. A short tribute film we'd ask the Sabol boys to put together over at NFL Films. That shouldn't cost too much. Maybe fifty grand. A hundred tops. They'd be happy to do it. Frank Gifford would narrate it, and he'd probably do it gratis. Then maybe a discussion, a reminiscence. The guys in leather chairs on a stage. Persian rugs. Humidors. We'd sell it to Fox Sports, maybe the NFL Network. ESPN or ESPN Classic. Maybe even HBO. I'd produce it if I could help. I could even come up with a ballpark budget if he gave me a couple minutes.

When I got through, Hanlon blinked at me and said, "We'll do sump'n."

The home game against Tampa, old-timers day, arrived with even less fanfare than Hanlon had suggested it might.

"I'm thinking of taking the bus," I said to my brother several times after he'd called and said he'd scrounged tickets for himself and my nephew Geoffrey so that all three of us could be at the game.

"I think I'll drive, Babe," he said.

He wanted to buy beers. Hero sandwiches. My big brother wanted to tailgate. And when he wanted to do something, I inevitably tagged along. I was a decent athlete in school, but he was always just a little bit better.

I told him the bus was convenient. That I needed to be there early because the '56 Giants were assembling for a pregame lunch I was hoping to get into.

"The bus lets you off right near where I can get my press credential," I said.

"I think I'll drive," he said.

I said, "The bus means you really don't have to fight traffic. The traffic jams getting into the parking lot are murder. They don't have a clue about getting cars in and out here. Back in L.A. we know how to do it."

But my brother insisted on driving. I thought I should tell him never mind, I'd stick with the bus. After all, I'm a middle-aged man in the process of making out my will. But of course, I didn't speak up.

A half an hour before the game started, as the '56 champions were wiping the last crumbs of cake from their mouths with their napkins at luncheon's end, I was sitting in my brother's Jeep FWD, stuck in line, waiting to pay for parking at Giants Stadium.

We finally parked the Jeep in a space next to a construction site about as far away from the stadium as my wife was from me in our new California King, and I took about two hasty bites of what would have been a great hero sandwich if I hadn't found myself pulling seagull feathers from my mouth because the birds were flapping and dive-bombing so intensely the air was thick with floating gull down and plummeting droppings.

"Where the heck were you?" I heard when I got to the press box less than fifteen minutes before kickoff.

It was the Giants' PR director, Peter John-Baptiste. He wore a big frown.

"We fixed it up so you could be at the luncheon," he said. He'd obviously gone to lengths. Maybe not great lengths, but me questioning how long those lengths were was only going to get him even more irritated. And he looked very irritated. Not ready to punch me in the nose, but he might have, I suppose, had John Mara not made it known throughout the organization that if anyone was going to bust me one it was going to be him, so everyone else had better lay off.

There was no way to explain to the irritated PR man what had happened. No way to tell him I'd just been at my own old-timers game, out in the parking lot. Where I'd reenacted that time half a century ago when I could stand on my head and insist, but if my big brother decided a thing was going to be done his way, that's the way it got done. No way to tell him that I was far more disappointed than he that I'd missed lunch.

I sat in the press box seething, a fifty-plus-year-old man furious over being deprived of something by his big brother, the way I could recall seething about other things my big brother used to deprive me of, like, say, the last cupcake in the box, or my father. Angrier, though, at myself. For feeling helpless and for having come to old-timers day acting as if not a day had passed since I'd haplessly cast hooks into my head while fishing with my brother.

My mood wasn't helped watching the Giants allow Tampa Bay to make a game of it. Either way, that worthy advisory, "No cheering in the press box," the admonition to divest yourself of all emotion, has always asked of me something I feel I ought to be able to—but somehow never can—muster: equanimity. How do you squelch the instinct to identify with something outside yourself? And if you can't help rooting, how do you get a grip? Especially on a day like today, which was so fraught.

At halftime, nine stories below, a group of aging men walk out onto the field, their limbs and joints aching in a way Tiki wants desperately to avoid. It is impossible for me to sit still, to remain unmoved. I don't know what this is, whether it's "cheering" or Restless Leg Syndrome, but whatever it is, I have to get out of my chair in the press box and stretch my legs.

I take the elevator down to field level. And instead of turning toward the lockers, the way reporters always do, I turn right and hotfoot down the corridor toward the east end zone. Although I have a credential, I keep my head down and my gaze averted from any security guards or police who are stationed along the way, hoping not to arouse their interest or enable them to latch on to me with a question like, "Where do you think you're going?" I had no answer to that question. Somehow I knew my credential wasn't good for where I was going.

Surrounding the portal, some standing at the divide between

the shadow of the stands and the brilliantly sunlit field, many women waited. They clutched at sweaters against a wind they weren't quite sheltered from and that found them at the end of the stadium in the dark recesses. They looked with pride out upon the field at the warriors their men had been. And some of them held coats, which the men they were waiting on had given them to hold as they walked out for the ceremony, wanting, as men, to appear to be as impervious to the elements as possible.

I hustled onto the field toward the 50-yard line. No one stopped me, so I kept going to the spot where the old-timers, the '56 Giants, had been positioned for a photograph. There was Sam Huff. Frank Gifford. Alex Webster. Andy Robustelli. Linebackers Harland Svare and Cliff Livingston. Receivers Bob Schnelker and Ken MacAfee. And the placekicker Ben Agajanian, who scored 11 points in the championship game. They'd had a private dinner at the 21 club the night before. Now a few photographers snapped away. A few people from the Giants' public events office were scattered around. No klieg lights. No velvet ropes. No limousines.

It was disappointing to me that this was treated as just another promotion. It was over in five minutes. The photos had been taken. The old-timers, the men who built the league, began to disperse. Some walked slowly, looking down, whether out of the habit enforced by old age or savoring one last time watching their own feet lay low the grass on a Giants field. Or perhaps they were reconjuring the way the earth felt shuddering against them fifty years ago when they, in sneakers, were champs in the snow.

Gifford, who was sitting, stands and runs his hand down his still-trim belly, and then he flashes a glance up at the range of stands, piled almost to the sky with cheering people. He's not wistful. He's just reminding himself what it looks like, checking to make sure it looks the same. It does.

I had last seen Gifford with Fred Exley in L.A. in 1987 for Super Bowl XXI. He'd agreed to meet Exley for a magazine story at the Beverly Wilshire Hotel by the pool. Their moments by the pool paraphrased all of their encounters—the celestial bemused by the astronomer, and ultimately, suffering himself to be looked at.

"How're you doin', Freddy?" Gifford said.

Gifford's eyes quickly measured Exley. It was a tic of Gifford's, maybe the result of years of sizing up tacklers, maybe not wanting people to get too big in front of him. He was always alert to menace.

"I'm doin' okay, Frank," Exley managed to mumble.

Just inside, through a sliding door and beyond billowing, pale white curtains within Gifford's hotel suite, we'd passed the tornadoed bedclothes that testified to the raw male fierceness of his lovemaking. He'd recently been remarried, to the beautiful entertainer Kathie Lee, and one supposed the sight of a sumptuous king-size bed covered in Egyptian cotton inside an all-expenses-paid private suite at the BW had offered an irresistible goad for the newlyweds' sport. And somehow forcing Frank Gifford to put off another round in the sheets for thirty minutes with a drunk could be construed as justifiable cause for a man to be stingy with his time.

But Frank Gifford, although he was nonplussed by Exley's attention from the moment he heard about the manuscript of *A Fan's Notes* from Bennett Cerf at a cocktail party, though he thinks of it to this day as a form of stalking, never failed to treat Fred Exley with mystified courtesy.

"Freddy, why're you drinking so much?" Frank asked.

"Ahhh. . . . y'know . . . Frank. . . ."

Gifford stayed on Exley. Told him to get off the booze.

Exley didn't. But Gifford still looks fit to this day, years later, standing in the sunshine at midfield in the Meadowlands at old-timers day. He doesn't need the help of a golf cart to make it around the way some of the others do, and if he did, probably wouldn't have showed up. Two old ex-teammates have to grip former Georgia Tech All-America lineman Ray Beck by the elbows and gently lift and drag his frail frame backward to a steady-enough sitting position on the rear of a golf cart. Next to him they prop his oxygen bottle. The other carts' seats fill, the drivers looking over their shoulders at impatient intervals to gauge when the load can be driven off so the second half can begin.

But I'm not going to let the second half begin until I get to meet a man sitting there in his eighties with thinning, wavy gray hair and round, shadowed eyes. His shoulders are wide and sloped.

"Mr. Robustelli," I say, and introduce myself as the person with whom he'd spoken on the phone a few times. The person who hadn't gotten to meet him and sit down next to him at lunch because he'd been stuck in a traffic jam with his big brother in his big gas guzzler. Responding, Robustelli accepts my hand to shake.

"You remember my name?" I ask him.

"Sure. How ya doin'?" Robustelli says.

His grip envelops mine. Big. Rough. I think at that moment I was a boy again. I feel an exquisite pain, one whose recollection moves me to tears.

"Whose idea was it to wear sneakers in the Bears game?" I ask nobody in particular. The former linebacker Cliff Livingston thinks it over. Livingston is bald, looks a step or two slower and wears a stud in his left ear. He regards me for a second, mentally sorting through stuff before shaking his head that he doesn't remember, which is—no shame in it—probably the way he shakes his head about more and more stuff lately. He looks like he is still tough as shit.

"Don't you remember, it was Andy's," the old lineman Gerry Huth pipes up, still ruddy-faced, with an offensive lineman's swayback and stovepipe legs and looking like he's learned a little bit about the best defense, too, which is laughing at it all.

"Andy had a sporting goods store and he brought 'em in, all those boxes." Huth enjoys a ripe chuckle, the kind you have at the memory of having outfoxed someone. "The Bears couldn't do a damn thing. Lombardi had us running like a machine. Mel Triplett hit one of those guys and knocked him on his ass. The Bears couldn't even stand up."

"Once a Giant," Livingston says, "always a Giant."

The gaze of the cart driver has now turned upon me, telling me it is time to stand back. The flatbed carts are filled. He is ready to ferry the men. I am holding them up.

I stand back and the carts smoothly roll away down the long, curved, deserted tunnel, into the shadows, silently, removing from my view the '56 Giants and, one last time, my father.

Chapter 7

Third-and-22

Iwas personally recruited to play football by the athletic
director and head coach of one of the premier schools in
the country.

This statement, while entirely factual, perhaps warrants
some qualification. The four-year institution of higher learning was and is *premier*—but not in football.

In cricket.

In football, my alma mater, Haverford College, with a
student body of fewer than eight hundred at the time and
founded by Quakers, was singularly inept.

But I *was* recruited. In 1968, Coach Dana Swan asked if
I wanted to come out for the team after its record went to
0–5 and he'd seen me make a cunning pass interception in an
intramural game. I never played. But it may have been upon

The immortal "LT," as in Limitless Testosterone. PETER READ MILLER hearing word of Swan's act of desperation that shortly there-after the Board of Managers voted to stop playing the sport, a decision that made recruiting top football talent, always a challenge, even harder, and from which, sad to say, the foot-ball program has never recovered.

Until then, Haverford played against schools like Juniata. You'd watch the competition file off the bus and most of the players looked as if they'd just been pulled out of a mine shaft after spending twelve hours in blackness swinging a pick against a seam of anthracite. I imagined they had all been told, once they'd worked their shifts, to gather around the mine boss by the paymaster's office, and the mine boss had something like this to say:

"Men, I know you've put in a long day. You work hard, long hours. Seventy, eighty hours a week a mile down in the ground, breathing coal dust and kerosene fumes that coat your lungs and kill you young, before you have a chance to see your kids grow'd. I know you don't get paid spit. Two bits an hour. Some of you who've lasted, a buck and a quarter. But that's not pay enough to live a decent life. To buy food for your family. To put clothes on your back. To pay for your kids' schoolbooks. I know you watch your fathers and brothers and uncles die young, choking on their own blood in the mines. Or going off overseas to fight in the military. And you watch your women grow old and gray years before their time, stealin' looks out their parlor curtains to see if their man's come home alive after his shift.

"It ain't much of a life. It's hell on earth. That's the way it's always been. And, let's face it, there ain't much that's gonna improve that. There ain't enough aspirin. Nobody's kiddin' anybody here. But maybe this can ease the pain. . . ."

Here is where the boss tears the cloth off a map on an easel behind him. It reveals Eastern Pennsylvania. The northeast coal region in detail. And lower down is a quarter-inch-wide red dot and next to where it says "Philadelphia" is the name of a town none of the miners has heard of. The boss picks up a pointer and gives that red dot a spank.

"This right here's a place, fellas," he says, "where boys no better'n you have it the opposite. A huge meal's put in front of 'em three times a day. All they want. A guy in a white chef's hat carvin' thick, juicy slices off a roast beef, puttin' it on their plates . . . all the gravy they want. Seconds, too. Every week, cleaning ladies do their linens, make their beds, sweep up, tidy till it's neat as a pin. They're boys, same as you. Only difference is, they'd soil theirselves if you told 'em they'd have to spend a single minute down in one of them mines you just came out of. Your life is hell—and theirs is heaven. Now I can't do anything about that. All I can tell you is this town's called Haverford . . . and in this town they got a college and most of the boys who go there wear their hair longer'n your girlfriend.

"Like I said, I can't do anything about your life, but I can tell you that if you maybe want to feel a little bit better about it for a couple hours, anybody feels like teaching these pot-smoking, draft-dodging puny faggots who is and who is not a red-blooded American man with a red-blooded American dick big enough for a bald eagle to perch on, climb into that bus over there and we'll go play ourselves a football game against Haverford College."

Highly motivated was what the Juniatas of the Haverford schedule looked like when they stomped off the bus, shaking the ground with enough force to rattle your love beads. The next few hours were just Haverford trainers running out onto the field and bending down over some prone former Merit Scholar from Sidwell Friends School who had already been accepted into the MD-PhD program at Yale and saying, "I think we may have to immobilize thy neck."

I suppose I'm thinking about my own school days because I'm taking my daughter to tour a new high school she's applying to. My wife's next to me.

"What question do *you* want to ask, Dad?"

My daughter is sitting in the backseat of the Prius.

"Question?"

"Yeah. Mom has her question she wants me to ask them, I have my question. What do you want to know about the school? Did you have time in New York to think up *your* question?"

"Make sure they have a good football team," I say.

"What?! Dad, I'm not going out for the football team."

The wife delivers one of her withering stares, the kind that leaves you looking for a tourniquet, and, turning to my daughter, says:

"Don't listen to your father. He's lost his marbles. All he can think about is what happened in the Chicago game. *The Chicago game . . . woe is me . . . the Chicago game . . .* And if it's not the Chicago game it's Tiki Barber and football. He can't think about anything else. He can't think about what schools you should go to, he can't think about getting the wooden gate fixed, he can't think about paying the electrical bill. All he can talk about is the Chicago game. . . ."

"If they have a good football team, it'll be a very smart school. Football players are smart," I say.

"You're insane. The ones who carry guns through airports? The ones shooting people in nightclubs, they're smart, huh?"

That's what I've been finding out during my season with the Giants. The stereotype of great football players being something less than intellectually gifted couldn't be further from the truth. Football players are by far the smartest pro athletes. In fact, they're smarter than just about any other group of professionals you could be around, like, for example, in my case, writers.

Do you know how smart you have to be to play in the National Football League? This is a cadre of about fifteen hundred individuals who, to a far greater extent than the rest of us smug assholes could ever hope to tolerate, live a working life of constant study and analysis of film, repetition in practice drills, fierce and untoward physical circumstance, intense focus and relentless critique of performance down to the most minute detail.

In short, there's not an oak-paneled boardroom or underground command bunker in this world with people sharper than the men sudsing their balls in an NFL shower.

"Do you have any idea how smart someone like Mathias Kiwanuka is?" I say to my wife and daughter. "He went to Boston College, okay? His grandfather was the prime minister of Uganda. He studied like crazy in college, but nothing like he studies now. He told me."

I tell them how Tiki Barber is never without a book. He and his twin brother, Ronde, the standout Tampa Bay defensive back, have coauthored children's books that Archie Manning reads at bedtime to his son Cooper's kids. Over the summer, Tiki was reading a fat history book about Korea, a subject close to his heart because his wife Ginny's parentage is Asian. Then it was *Culture Warrior*, Bill O'Reilly's book. Mid-season, no sooner than word's out that this is his last roll of the dice before heading to the cashier's window with his chips, Tiki's flaunting a much-thumbed paperback on the life of Jim Brown.

Look around the locker room. Stanford. Rutgers. Notre Dame. Michigan. USC. Penn. Columbia. Michigan State. Virginia. Pro players are nearly all college graduates. More than other professional athletes. And not all the schools, nor their classes, are the jokes people unthinkingly assume they are. Let's put it this way: I wouldn't want to have to compare the number of days I was a no-show at class to that of any of these guys.

What separates winners from losers is what they've got going on upstairs. The ability to focus. "If you want to win in the playoffs," Tiki says, "the team that makes the least mistakes wins. Period. Period, that's it. Because everybody is good at that point. You have been through the season, you've gone through your ups and downs, bumps and bruises, you know what you're good at. The teams that make the least mistakes in the playoffs win, period. It's not the better team, it's who makes the least mistakes."

That's where the wear and tear is when you are really on the line. When a group of people have to execute something perfectly for a few seconds, like a well-coordinated cast and crew. It's all going on film. It's forever. It's camera-ready. And it's being performed live. Blocking a multicamera sitcom on stage can get complicated, but not as complicated as blocking the Bears. Your moves have got to be precise. In the six thousand square yards of chaos that amounts to a National Football League soundstage, if you are one foot off your mark at any given moment—if, for example, you misremember your cue: which shoulder to turn toward camera, say, or the play called in the huddle as "44 Bob" rather than "45 Bob"—you will take your first step the wrong way, as Tiki did on one crucial play, and screw up the handoff from Eli, resulting in a fumble against the Colts late in the third quarter. Or if a sure touchdown pass to Jeremy Shockey is thrown not to his right shoulder, but six inches to the inside where a defender can reach and knock it down near the goal line and you have to settle for a field goal, as happened at home in the rematch against Dallas—you've ruined the take, blown your line in the scene, screwed up what you needed to do, and you'll lose. And, as Tim Mara used to say, "Only the winner goes to dinner."

And mental mistakes are killing the Giants. It leads to a Monday night loss in Jacksonville on November 20. And the very next Sunday against the Titans, who come from behind after being down by twenty-one points.

The losses taught me one thing. There is this difference between the thirteen-year-old I am now and the thirteen-year-old I once was: Back then, losing on a last-second kick would tear me up. Now, it is the slower, more agonizing losses that are toughest to tolerate. You come to it all with decades' less faith. And much tougher skin. The sudden jolt is just an abrupt horror like so many you're already old enough to have faced. Or perhaps that's just another way of saying that with age comes the loss of the ability to feel things keenly. In my case now, it is the slow, relentless dwindling that I most bemoan.

That was what made the Tennessee game so insufferable. I'd sat down in a neighborhood bar near my house in Santa Monica. I ordered a beer and asked them to turn on the Giants game.

The bartender said, "I don't think that's going to be possible."

I said, "Oh, really"—and here I made a several-second, look-over-both-shoulders show of scanning the joint. There were maybe 350 TV monitors in the place. More than you'd find in Best Buy. At the rate we're going, within twenty years 35 percent of the earth's surface is going to be covered in plasma screens—"is that so? I see a lot of TV in here."

He said, "This is a New England Patriots bar."

"Just put it on one screen then," I said.

"I don't think so."

That's when someone else came over, put down the draft beer I'd ordered, stood back and scribbled out a check. He casually slapped it on the counter in front of me and moved his hand toward the $20 bill I'd placed there. But I slapped my hand on the bill and, possibly, several of his fingers, yelling:

"Nope. I'm not paying for this. Not if I can't watch the Giants game."

The bartender said, "You ordered the beer, didn't you?"

I turned. Three towering guys in Tom Brady, Richard Seymour and Ted Bruschi jerseys were glowering at me.

"What's the problem, bud?" Tom Brady wanted to know. The towering Richard Seymour shifted his weight from foot to spoiling foot. He had a bristly short red mustache and clenched his fist behind his back while eyeing the bridge of my nose.

"If I can't watch the goddamn Giants game, I'm not paying for the goddamn beer," I announced. This was (a) right in Tom Brady's and Richard Seymour's and Teddy Bruschi's faces; and (b) loud enough so everyone in the bar could hear it.

Everyone stopped speaking. I realized I had just told a barful of angry men to go fuck themselves. I felt a momentary, inward glow. I was proud of myself. How many guys with a master's in English lit from Columbia do that? Not too many. At least, none who lived to tell the tale. I felt like I was edging out on some ledge.

Which was when I realized I better start edging for the door.

"What're you, some kinda proud Giants fan or something?" Teddy Bruschi said with a leer.

"Jerk," I heard from somewhere.

Richard Seymour advanced.

I got outside and soon Richard Seymour and Teddy Bruschi and several other Patriots clotted the threshold, regarding me angrily.

But they were on the horns of a dilemma. Enjoy whaling on me or miss the Patriots' kickoff. The fact that they were such big fans saved my life, and I watched them return inside as soon as they heard the ref's whistle on the TV. I felt my heart pounding. And again, as was happening from time to time lately, I caught myself short. I thought, Since when did "bar fight" get put on my to-do list? Why was I suddenly going around asking for it? I never go around asking for it.

A few blocks down the street was another bar. It had beer and TV, too, and that's where I watched with my buddy Brock. When the Giants got out in front by twenty-one, leaving me so utterly sated with satisfaction that I could hardly move . . . a crazy, insidious thought wormed its way into my head: I'd return to that Patriots bar I'd first been forced out of, throw open the front door, and flip the crowd of Patriots fans my middle finger.

Within seconds I returned to rationality. *What is this all about?* I thought. What sort of perversity is at work here?

What does it say about someone that he has escaped a mob beating and now wants to court another?

I recalled that moment in the Clarion Hotel of Albany months earlier. Where I'd realized I'd gone too far laying claim to a silly plastic Giants press credential. Then, I'd had the sense of being shaken by the shoulders, a better self cautioning me to watch my step. But I'd pushed that arm aside and gone on. This felt like that. Don't go back to that bar. You're asking for it.

Nevertheless, I finished my beer and got set to leave.

My determination to "show them" was a clear sign I had lost my wits—but before I got out the door, and with the Titans facing a make-or-break fourth down, the Giants' rookie defensive end Kiwanuka lost his. He bolted into the Tennessee backfield and wrapped quarterback Vince Young up to sack him—helmet square on Young's chest—and close out the game and then, unbelievably, inexplicably, released his grip. Let Young go. Young said thank you and ran for a first down and, subsequently, the Titans overcame that twenty-one-point deficit and won.

It is the biggest fourth-quarter meltdown in the history of the team. "Knockin' on Heaven's Door" began playing in my head. A Higher Being was sending me a message at this moment. Kiwanuka's nonsack was a fork in the road for me. Down one road the Giants won and I returned to that bar and got the shit kicked out of me. But the Higher Being said it was going to spare me from going back to that bar and getting that beating. The Higher Being pried Kiwanuka's arms apart and sent me down that other road. He spared me a beating. Turned out, he had something worse in store.

Kiwanuka later explained that he didn't finish the tackle because he thought Young had thrown the ball and didn't want to be penalized for roughing the passer. The reason that relenting was in his mind even as every muscle in his body tensed to deliver a coup de grâce to Young was that Kiwanuka had been called for a roughing-the-passer penalty the week before in the loss against Jacksonville (another of those nagging little mental mistakes).

It seemed sadly ironic that such an intelligent player would be penalized for thinking too much. And yet would be shown to have so much learning to do. Kiwanuka is enormously fast, all overacute angles, like a picture of wind-swift pursuit you'd find in a cave painting. At first, over the summer, I watched him take a running start from as far back as ten yards away, lower his shoulders, fork his upper torso forward and slam pad-first straight into a blocker—almost like a ram bounding across a meadow and slamming horns into a rival. But despite the foot-pounds that generates, this so-called bull rush is not his game. His game is speed, so much so that the Giants have some defenses in which he drops back into pass coverage. Some teams with truly fast defensive ends such as Kiwanuka do this, although I'm not sold on the concept. Sure, it's showy—look at us, our ends are so quick they can cover—and, it must be granted, it's confusing. Early in the season, dropping off the line, Kiwanuka— you could almost see the quarterbacks asking, *"Where the hell did he come from?"*—grabbed two interceptions and took one back almost to the end zone.

Despite this, I'm not sure how a six-five lineman in a three-point stance suddenly having to straighten up and backpedal, locate his man, and pursue him is your best means of pass coverage.

Case in point: the Giants' very first game, against the Colts. Less than three minutes to go in the first half, third and goal on the Giants 2-yard line, Peyton Manning completed a TD pass to his tight end Dallas Clark, on a throw to the far corner of the end zone. It put Peyton 13 points up on Eli.

Michael Strahan, the Giants' DE and, along with Tiki, the team's twin pillars of Hercules, seemed to have pass-coverage responsibilities. Coming out of his stance, Strahan felt Clark go by him, wheeled, and took off full-tilt in pursuit. But Clark had come off the line and was already a step into the end zone before Strahan could finish swiveling to begin that pursuit. And that one step was enough. Clark caught Manning's pass over his shoulder for 6 just before Strahan could reach him and drag him down.

Strahan is the last link to the Lawrence Taylor era. LT's final year, 1993, was Strahan's rookie season. He is in the royal bloodline. He is a first-ballot future Hall of Famer. Yet my respect for the all-out effort Strahan gives on every play grew more immense watching this simple 2-yard pass. Strahan hadn't a prayer that Peyton Manning's pass would be over- or underthrown; no, this pass would drop, perfectly arched, spiraling tightly, right into Dallas Clark's arms for a touchdown.

That's got to leave your hope and effort a little malnourished. Knowing right away that the ball will be there. You can almost see the words, "Oh, shit," flash across Strahan's face when he realizes Clark's his man.

I have no idea how he can even have his mind on the game. His ex-wife, Jean, spent all summer in divorce court paintballing Strahan, insinuating he was gay and referring to his "alternative lifestyle," which everyone assumed meant the

Giants had a future Hall of Fame Sodomite, a notion that must have sent Wellington Mara into a crocodilian death spin in his grave. She insisted, though, that she only meant that Strahan was merely an adulterer, a liar, and a sex fetishist. And after all that his wife walks away with sixteen mil and 18K a month in child support.

My mind wouldn't be on the game. I've been slimed, called some kind of sex deviant and pretty much totally deranged, half my money's gone and on top of that, now I'm supposed to stop a perfect Peyton Manning pass, playing this dumb defense down on our own 2-yard line. . . . Go fuck yourself, I might very well be thinking, I'm gonna go take a stroll on the boardwalk.

Not Strahan. However discouraged all of that might have made him, he knew his only chance of causing an incomplete pass and forcing the Colts to settle for a field goal was to make sure that Clark dropped the ball.

Strahan never let up. Even though he knew he'd never get there in time. And when the pass from Peyton Manning did float as beautifully as you knew it would right into Clark's hands so that Clark didn't just catch, he accepted the ball the way you would a baby tossed from a window in a fire, Strahan pounced like a beast of prey on his back. He nearly ripped Clark's legs out of their sockets and Clark smacked down so hard face-first into the ground, he bounced.

Clark held on to the ball. But when he got back to the sidelines I'm willing to bet he had a couple of blades of Giants Stadium's synthetic FieldTurf stuck in his mouth and nose.

Maybe Kiwanuka could have gotten back there faster than Strahan. He probably could have. Maybe he could have stopped that touchdown. I don't think there's anything

Kiwanuka won't wind up being able to do on a football field, including playing safety. That's how fast he is.

Kiwanuka's A move is that turbocharged outside rush that enabled him to get around lumbering left tackles in the ACC conference about as easily as the Germans outflanked the French Army. But in the NFL one strength alone becomes one-dimensional. And such is the competitive intensity of the league that if you have only one strength, that strength will become a weakness.

And so it was that the Giants' season began to fall apart when Chicago's offense broke its huddle and came to the line of scrimmage at its own 30-yard line with 1:30 left in the first half and trailing the Giants, 13–3, on the evening of Sunday, November 12. And a series of what Lemony Snicket might call "unfortunate events" befell the football Giants. They had already suffered key injuries to LeVar Arrington in the win against Dallas; to All-Pro defensive end Osi Umenyiora the next week in the win against Tampa Bay; and to both All-Pro defensive end Michael Strahan and the team's career leader in receptions, the inestimable Amani Toomer, in the win against Houston the week after that.

But it was in the Chicago game the following week that the Giants turned into Humpty Dumpty.

It was third down.

This November matchup between the two teams was just the latest whiskey bottle to the head in a bar fight that's been raging for eighty-one years. It's kind of like when John Wayne and Lee Marvin met up in the movies—whenever and wherever it happened to be; Hawaii or Dodge City—they quickly got down to scuffling. The Giants' collective front-office memory recalls to this day that in earlier years, after it became business practice for teams to swap game films with their upcoming opponents, Halas's can of acetate would arrive at the Giants' office on 42nd Street (before the move to Columbus Circle) with all the Bears' scoring plays edited out so the Giants wouldn't get a peek.

And one play, of course, can live forever.

That one play can be good or bad. Over the years, the Giants have been, as the medics would say, "boxed" by several neck darts whose tips have been dipped in one drop of a rare spider venom that causes instant rigor mortis.

Three of the worst in the last few decades:

1. The fumble. 1978. Satan shows who's boss. Running out the clock against Philly. Pisarcik and Csonka mix up the handoff. Herm Edwards runs it back all the way and the Eagles win.

2. The snap. 2002. Satan shows he's still got it. Trey Junkins's crummy hike that screwed up a gimme Matt Bryant field goal that would have beaten the 49ers in the NFC wildcard game.

3. The kick. 2003. Satan letting you know you're still on his call list. The Giants take the lead with just eleven seconds left when Matt Bryant's out-of-bounds kickoff against Dallas allows the Cowboys to set up shop for a game-tying field goal and a win in OT.

But there have been some uncanny foul-ups against the Bears as well.

Like Sean Landeta whiffing on a punt in the 1985 playoff loss against Chicago.

The good thing, if a good thing can be said, about most such gaffes is that they come in crucial situations like the playoffs, and when they result in the Giants losing, at least the season is over. There are no more games. This game against Chicago in November didn't come with a couple quarters left in the year—it had an entire half a season stretched out in front of it to scald and mutilate.

Six and two over the first half of the schedule, and facing the once-beaten Bears for potential home-field advantage in the conference final, still nearly two months away.

It was third down.

One more play and the Bears would kick and the Giants would get a crack to march down the field and salt the game away before halftime.

Give your character a problem and you have the makings of a good script. That's what we had here because, for starters, that's the essence of what a third down is—confronting a problem.

Which was major: It was third-and-22.

Third downs are the hinges in the tale being told. The meat of the scene. The clash of intentions. Making it on third down creates a future. It keeps the drive alive. It continues the story. It keeps you in the scene. It keeps you breathing.

Of course, teams can convert third downs. Third-and-1. Third-and-4. Third-and-8. Third-and-15.

Third-and-22?

Chicago didn't pass, which might have seemed the likeliest choice to get such a huge chunk of yardage—nearly a quarter of the field—but it anticipated what kind of overenthusiastic burst off the line the Giants' young Kiwanuka would take in a pass rush, so, at the snap, when the rookie, making his first start replacing the injured Umenyiora, blasted off pell-mell upfield—and out of the play—he delivered himself right into Chicago's hands. I don't know for sure, of course, but they called the play exactly for this reason, it seemed.

Bears quarterback Rex Grossman calmly handed the ball off to Thomas Jones. Behind a wedge of linemen, Jones ran untouched for 26 yards before he trotted out of bounds with the first down. He could have put on a dress and skipped.

Thomas got four more than he needed and never got touched. Never had to pay for it.

As if to confirm how grievous this wound was to the team's GTP (Gross Testicular Product), Jay Feely came up short on a field goal later on and the Bears' Devin Hester caught it in the end zone, took a few lazy decoy steps until he was sure the Giants weren't paying any attention to him, then took off and sprinted down the sideline for a 108-yard touchdown return.

Two breakdowns like that in one game. Two a season, maybe. But two in one game? Chicago turned Giants Stadium into one big Turkish prison.

So began the Great Reversal. It washed through Jacksonville and crested with a third straight loss at the hands of Tennessee and Kiwanuka's Freudian slip against Vince Young.

Week in and week out, after the game, in the Giants locker room, each player said the same thing:

"I don't know why it keeps happening, and if I did know why, I'd go right to the coaches and tell them," the lineman, Kareem McKenzie, said.

"We talked all week about thinking of the circumstances and keeping our poise and controlling our emotions, but . . . ,"

Coughlin said over and over after every loss in his postgame press conference.

"As good a team as we were is as bad as we played this week," Tiki said. "We're faltering. We're wasting it."

"We've just got to play better," Eli said. "I've just got to go through my reads and find the open receivers. . . ."

Sometimes there are no reasons. You walk out of your building one morning, like Camus's Dr. Rieux did, and kick aside a dead rat lying in your doorway, and over the next few weeks the losses pile up as a plague overwhelms your community and then vanishes for no other reason than that it is done.

The team's followers claimed it was indeed a plague—of injuries. Strahan coming down wrong, suffering a Lisfranc sprain to his foot and missing the last half-year. Umenyiora gone, too. Arrington gone for the season in the first Dallas game with an Achilles. Pettigout, the all-important left tackle, gone with a broken foot, limping out of the locker room on crutches after the Bears game, in the midst of a credible season, having dispensed a not-always-great but nevertheless commendable eight years to the team, never to return. And, much too overlooked, but perhaps most important of all, the receiver, Amani Toomer, lost for the season with an improbable knee injury suffered simply while running a pass route against Houston without a finger ever touching him.

All these injuries gave the Giants possession issues. On defense they couldn't get the other team off the field. And they couldn't keep their own offense on the field when they needed to because Toomer, who offered Manning reassurance at third-down crunch time, wasn't there. Toomer, the man who caught the emotional, last-second touchdown pass that beat Denver in the last game Wellington Mara ever saw, the most undercelebrated player on the team, a calm, decent, consummate professional, was the player they missed the most. He would have made some plays.

Game after game turned into a losing story: scoring too few points because they settled for field goals, allowing the opponent to come down the field in the fourth quarter and snatch the prize when the defense failed.

How could that happen?

"I think we have a chance to be a defense for the ages," LeVar Arrington had said in the summer. That was around the time Will Demps, the new safety from Baltimore—a defense with a reputation for savagery rivaled only by the Russian mob—joined the team, and punctuated his arrival by giving Shockey a concussion in a non-contact practice that was, I thought, definitely meant to second Arrington's motion.

It's all so very hard to reconcile. How could they fall apart this way? How could it have come to this?

You're sitting here in the admissions office. Your daughter's gone in to "have a chat" with a pleasant school official. There's a fire in the fireplace. Your wife is beside you. And the look on her face tells you she feels good. Sure, this "interview" stuff is no fun. But can you believe we've gotten this far? From that little baby . . . to now? That mature young woman we just saw walk away to be interviewed, carrying herself with such presence?

"Aren't we lucky," that look says.

I'm thinking I could be at the airport in Burbank and on a plane back East, and I'd get into Newark and I'd rent a car. And somehow or other—it shouldn't be too hard, I remember the name of his business; it was Fusco Electrical Supply—I could be knocking on Sam Fusco's door somewhere in suburban New Jersey in, oh, eight hours. You remember—the guy with the short bus. Painted blue. Giants blue. I'd skip out on my life here—maybe take the script for the TV pilot I was writing—and move in with Sam Fusco. He would understand me because he had once burned a Redskins jersey in his yard. He would take me in, no questions asked. His wife, or whoever he lived with, a good woman, I'm sure, would probably be a little upset with her husband for letting me move in with them and live upstairs. But in the end Sam would convince her it was just the next latest craziest Giant fan thing to do. The latest in a lifetime of inexplicable, harebrained Giants things Sam's done and that she's somehow put up with. She's put up with all the others. And she'll put up with this.

Besides, I'd say if there was any wavering at the front step, "I can always help out in the store. Please. You don't understand. I can't go back to my normal life. I can't be a thirteen-year-old boy stuck in a middle-aged man's body anymore. My body won't take it. It's giving out. I'm throbbing and twitching. And my mind can't take it anymore. I can't sleep. You must understand, Mrs. Fusco—you've lived with Sammy all these years. Please let me stay!"—

"Look at this," my wife says. She's holding a school brochure under my nose. "Patty Kanicki's kid goes here."

"Mmhm."

—I'd learn those electrical supply store shelves by heart. Every size socket. Screws. Clamps. Top to bottom. I'd live upstairs in Sam Fusco's house and pay it off by working in his store and on Sundays we'd drive the Touchdown Express Bus to the Meadowlands and park and grill and drink. It made sense.

Sam would understand what it felt like after the way they lost on a last-second field goal to Dallas at home just six weeks after beating them in Texas. And wearing their red jerseys! Their war jerseys. The ones they wear once a year. The one Wellington Mara brought to heaven with him because God wanted to check it out. It's the only red He allows in heaven.

The Giants brought the red uni back in 2004 after having not worn red in over half a century. When, once a year, they appear in the Giants red, the earth shivers. It stirs visions of Hinkey Haines catching that pass tossed off the Radiator Building overlooking Bryant Park; of George Preston Marshall marching his Washington Redskins band down Broadway when Sammy Baugh came to town; of a family that stayed the course right to the altar at St. Patrick's. It reminds you of rain-washed nights, the traffic pouring uptown, past all the sawdust on the floors of all those bars, past P. J. Clarke's, where the ghosts of every player sit with a beer and a burger.

They lost to Dallas in that jersey! The stress is unhealthy. Nonfat milk and high-fiber cereal mean nothing against four straight losses. The team being 6–6. Back at .500. Mediocrity. Maybe missing the playoffs. Tiki not even making the play-offs. No, Sam Fusco is going to have to take me in—

"The Vaughns' kid too," my wife says, pointing at a photo on another page of the school brochure. "Look at this beautiful new theater they built."

"Mmhm."

—Because it can't go on like this. I can't live this life when this life is living me. And if it is going to live me, I better live it with Sam Fusco. My shot at sanity has turned into a third-and-22. I'll tell my wife.

"We need to talk," I blurt out.

"Go ahead," she says, putting down the school brochure. It's very peaceful inside the little office with the little fire burning behind us.

I clear my throat and say, "It's about football."

She starts to groan but sees I'm serious and stops herself.

"Actually, it's about more than football," I say.

"You didn't get into another bar fight, did you?"

"I didn't get into a bar fight," I say.

I want to get this out right. It's turning out to be harder than I thought, being a kid again. And this close-up look at what it was like wasn't doing my nerves any good. It probably wasn't doing too much good for the marriage, either. After taking a deep breath I say:

"Do you understand the concept of downs?"

Her mouth crumples and she says, "You know that's always been a tough one for me. 'Down' sounds bad, but it's good, right?"

"Think of it as a 'try,' okay? Each team gets four 'tries.' "

"Okay. But do you want to make a down or not?" she says.

"You want to make a first down."

"Why don't you want to make a second down?"

"The point is you get first down and then second down, but the down where you really have to make something happen is third down. Third down is crucial, see? All of life is about third down."

"All of life?" she says.

"Metaphorically. Do you understand the concept of third-and-long?"

"Third and a long number of yards that you have to make to get to ten."

"Yeah, now think about this: Do you understand the concept of third-and-22?"

"I thought you only needed ten."

"So you don't understand the concept of third-and-22?"

"I'm trying to, sweetie pie. It obviously means something important. That's a lot of yards for a team to have to get, is that what you're trying to say?"

"Yes. Third-and-22 is impossible. No team makes it on third-and-22. It can't happen. It's out of the question. Oh, never mind. I could go over there and pick up the phone and call the Elias Sports Bureau—you know, the place in New York where they keep all the statistics—and if I asked them, 'All of last year, how many times did a team make it on third-and-22?' I guarantee you they would say, 'Only once. One time.' "

My wife draws back beyond spittle range and clicks her eyes toward the admissions assistant at the desk, whose mouth is open.

In response to my wife's reproachful look, I breathe deeply and sit back. I clam up. I'm behaving inappropriately. Maybe I've even hurt my daughter's chances of getting into this school. "Loud, obnoxious father brought office to a standstill" would probably be stapled as a note on my child's application.

But none of them gets it. No one has a clue. So stay in your room. Look at the wall. Play on the computer. Show up at mealtime. But understand that, like it was way back when, there is no use trying to explain yourself to the world, to the people around you: your wife, your child, your friends, your brother, anybody. Swim in it. Writhe in it.

It was third-and-22.

Will somebody please make a play?

Tiki Barber, "a Giant like no other." MICHAEL J. LEBRECHT II

Chapter 8

Tiki Barber Gets Dressed

Tiki Barber gets dressed. He drags a towel across his broad shoulders. His locker is right next to the showers. Beyond, there are echoes of shouts pitched high enough to be heard over the roar and splash of water. Teammates emerge from the clouds of steam, small towels held around their waists. A losing locker room is an ice box, but the Giants have just beaten the Redskins to get into the playoffs and it is *hot* in here.

A few feet away, Eli Manning, in boxers that look like they were picked off a charity table in a church basement, his hair a wet tangle, burnishes his growing reputation for being one of the city's least-colorful athletes:

"I think we did some good things out there tonight. . . ."

But Tiki is silent. He stares evenly and straight ahead into the locker. Just getting dressed. Like maybe he's thinking about something on the grocery list, or reminding himself he's got an appointment tomorrow morning for a massage at the Oasis day spa. As if he were at home, smoothing on some lotion, stepping into his clingy mid-thigh briefs. All by himself.

Just Tiki. Tiki's iPod. His overnight bag. And a book, *Washington's Spies.*

Tiki gets dressed.

No way is he five ten, as listed. If he's five nine, I'm a six-footer. The majesty of his body isn't its size, however hugely strong he is after years of exhausting, nearly year-round weight training; it's in its proportion. The man is compact. Tiki's leg ascend with sculpted might, and no doubt more than a few of the female journalists about, however impregnable their professional virtue, can't help but succumb to an appreciation of this perk in the job—watching Tiki Barber get dressed.

Barber pulls on his pants. Then his shirt, through which the few remaining wet spots he hasn't toweled off appear in damp blots below and behind his neck. His gaudiest accoutrement is usually his tie knot, and when he has secured yet another saucy, fat one into place, he tugs on his suit jacket and, now, shooting his cuffs, he turns.

Fifty people await him. They are pressed against the walls and sardined against the cinder blocks. Print reporters, TV broadcasters, pads and microphones and recorders and cameramen, male and female, have watched him saw the towel north and south a few times just like you do at home, then don his typically stylish suit. Some front office officials, traveling with the team, are also here looking on. Older men, effectively the team's deacons, with white hair, their palms pressed flat, stand inanimate against the wall. Solemnly attending.

The floor is strewn with towels and tape and crumpled gloves and eddies of steam and the exoskeletal-like remains of the discarded shoulder pads and helmets among the bulging duffels holding each player's gear. It's impossible to move. I am in the process of imagining I am a *Life* magazine photographer, shooting from out of the shower past Tiki's shoulder at all the people just standing there, particularly some nearby women, checking out Tiki's tiki, when there is a nod and then a bailiff-loud summons:

"Tiki's going to the podium." Peter John-Baptiste, the Giants' PR guy, announces.

"Tiki's going to the podium!" is picked up through the crowd. "Tiki's going to the podium!"

Barber wades through the throng in the visitors' locker room. Reporters and microphones and cameras surge after him in a steeplechase, hopping and tripping over the hurdle-high duffels, looking like wildlife fleeing a forest fire, banging at the other players' stools even as they balance a foot on them to lace up their shoes, or forcing other players who tower over the stampede to shrink back as they look down their noses to even up the tails of their shirts, their eyes following Barber while applying their massive hands to the tiny bottom buttons.

"Tiki's going to the podium."

Tiki "goes to the podium" to address the media after every game—he's central to the story. But consider how different it is from a week ago, when there was no carefree shouting coming from the showers and the team had put in its worst performance of the year. Which was saying something. Given Chicago. And Seattle. And Jacksonville. And Tennessee. And the return matches against Philadelphia and Dallas, both lost in the Meadowlands. Among all those, their greatest flop came against New Orleans on Christmas Eve, when they lost 30–7 and fell below .500.

What decent person could begrudge the Saints? Especially if you remembered the previous year when because of Hurricane Katrina the Saints were forced to play their "home game" against the Giants at the Meadowlands, where they were welcomed as storm survivors and then killed on the scoreboard.

"How fair was that?" I had asked Ernie Accorsi months earlier when I'd spoken to him in his office. It was simple justice, wasn't it, that the Giants volunteer to play this year's game down in the reopened Superdome? It would be a great gesture, something along the lines of this post-partisanship thing we've got going out in California thanks to Governor Arnold. Accorsi, girding for his final season as the GM, laughed, saw his leg wasn't being pulled and said:

"Fuck that."

In any event, the Giants did little to discourage the Saints from being highly motivated, the defense showing the same courtesy it had to so many other teams during the Great Reversal. The offense was true to fickle form. On the fourth play of the game, Manning threw a 55-yard touchdown pass to Burress, and no sooner had you finished cheering and whooping about that in your mind and sheepishly shrugging to yourself, reminding yourself not to get too carried away and thinking, I hope that's not the last points they score, than that became the veritable case.

The Giants never took a snap in Saints territory all game, which is evidence of enough team-wide bewilderment to get them tossed into the back of a city van and taken in for a psychiatric evaluation. Fans began yelling "Fire Coughlin" by the end of the first half.

Not just the fans but the beat writers were calling for Coughlin's head. That's how bad it got. It was back to the '60s and "Good-bye Allie." In the *Post*, Paul Schwartz said the team "just wasn't that good," and wrote, "The most glaring and potentially disturbing aspect to this season is the painfully slow, creep-forward, inch-backward development of Manning, who after 37 starts clearly is not as mentally sharp or as physically advanced as the Giants envisioned he'd be."

Manning's interception late in the Saints game wasn't critical to the final score—the game was already lost. But on the team's downward climb it set a shoeprint on a lower rung of futility—they were so bad they couldn't avoid misfortune even on meaningless plays. On Manning's last interception, the Saints' Jay Bellamy threw a block that dinged up Jeremy Shockey's ankle.

And, even worse than losing in their red jerseys, as they had against Dallas, if anything could be—this was Tiki Barber's last home game. One of his two boys, Chason, had accompanied him out to midfield for the coin toss.

The Giants walked off their home field for the last time that year. To recall them in their bold ranks on the green fields of summer as they hopped and stretched in the afternoon sunshine, and to then see them as they exited beaten and downtrodden in winter was to feel your heart crunched beneath an elephant's foot. The sorrow made you want to clap your hands over your ears.

Reporters typically descend to the field-level locker rooms

beginning five minutes before game's end. This requires a long trek from the elevator down the corridor, past where the players walk off the field and another twenty yards beyond to the press room, where Coughlin is available for questions before reporters are let into the nearby locker room to talk to the team.

But following the New Orleans game the reporters did not scurry to the interview room. Instead, they gathered in a knot in the tunnel where the players file off the field beneath the stands. For this game, the men and women who cover the Giants, and who had covered the team for ten years—from the *Times*, the *Post*, the *News*, the *Bergen Record*, the *Newark Star-Ledger*, *Newsday*, the *Hartford Courant*, and an assortment of sports Web sites—made a point of being at this spot to watch Tiki Barber come off the field.

This wasn't simply the obvious place for any journalist to be. It was the obvious place to be for anyone with a sense of the history of this football team and the history of the city. Of any place to be in the city of New York, or, clearly, at least to me, in the entire world at this moment, this was it. This was to be able to say to my grandchildren, "I was there when Tiki Barber came off the field for the last time." You should be able to say a couple of things like that to grandchildren, give them something to walk around the schoolyard with.

The "no cheering in the press box" rule extends everywhere (except to Philadelphia journalists), but even the toughest appeared tested not to betray the disappointment they felt for Tiki after this pig of a game against New Orleans. Surveying the grim set to their faces, one wondered whether, who knows, had things gone otherwise, had Tiki played the game he'd wanted and had the Giants won or at least not disgraced their uniform, some of the crustiest "scribes" might even have let out a terse final salute to the man Dave Anderson that week in the *Times* called "the best running back the Giants have ever had."

Then: Shockey!

No matter how tightly you might have clamped your ears shut from the sorrow in the wake of Tiki's last home game, it wouldn't have kept out the sound of Shockey sparking, white-hot, his mouth spitting like an acetylene torch. He was blistering Bellamy because a bum ankle might very well keep him out of next week's crucial game against Washington and it seemed like he was promising the Saints player who'd caused it that he'd soon be history.

"You will, motherfucker. You suck."

Shockey's words resounded as the players split apart and headed for their locker rooms. They accessed how everyone was feeling at the moment, which was lousy.

Tiki had shaken the last hand extended over the railing from the stands and smiled his last thanks before ducking into the tunnel. He had finished his public bows, given his cap to a girl in the stands and now, finally, no longer on display, he ducked into the tunnel and cracked with dismay. It was a rare parting of the curtain on this immaculate man. A small black cyclone is what I thought. Three large sweaty Giants linemen trundled ahead of him nonchalantly but, I'm sure, by design, as if drawn in a chalk talk, so that Tiki could do for one more time what he had done so well for ten years: follow his blockers, who shielded him from view and from the press. Tiki darted to the locker room without stopping. He didn't want to be seen this way. And the reporters on hand didn't want to have to see him that way. I felt my lips draw back tight in distaste of the sight.

I knew that Frank Gifford was upstairs watching the game. I had imagined a worthy adieu for Tiki, and perhaps Gifford himself descending to the locker room to bestow a "Good job, son" pat on the shoulder. After all, Gifford had taken a proprietary interest in Tiki, who was fumble-prone early in his career. Frank called Tiki to offer encouragement, to tell him not to let the setbacks linger. Frank took Tiki out to lunch and advised him on getting a career under way in the media. But plaudits weren't in the cards today. The team was "dejected" and "discouraged."

Those were Tiki's words after the game. After the cooling-off period, when he'd done what to me seemed the nearly superhuman mental bench-pressing required to have come off the field fuming as he did and then greet the press with equanimity mere minutes later. Tiki has Olympian strength of mind.

"We played hard, but we played stupid," he said. "And we made mistakes, and you can't win that way. We all know what we need to do, what we have to do—we're simply not doing it. We have one more game. It's against a division rival [Washington]. It's on the road. And we just need to play well. We need to remember the fundamentals. Simplicity. Not trying to analyze this game as rocket science or something extremely complex. It's about putting on your pads. Play hard, first and foremost, and doing what we've been doing since we were twelve years old. Running. Tackling. Blocking. Catching. As we approach our last game we have to correct it."

Coughlin was outwardly oblivious to the chants for his head and seemed to have had a fine Christmas ("I got a nice shirt, some slippers, that kind of stuff," he told me, "and some books. *Mayflower.* And that book about *Unitas.*"). But there was no mistaking the rage that encompassed New York. The headlines made your blood curdle.

"It's Christmas and everyone wants to be merry," Shaun O'Hara said, mirroring Big Blue Nation's glum mood, "but it's hard to be merry when you play like we did."

The rage built to a point where Stephen Mara—one of Wellington's sons who isn't even involved with the team; he's a stockbroker—lost it on the floor of the New York Stock Exchange. A colleague he'd known for years, a fifty-seven-year-old grandfather named Bob Tomasulo, an Eagles fan, greeted him with a jibe one Monday morning after the team's 36–22 loss at home to Philly.

Mara went berserk.

"I'm gonna fucking kill you," Stephen Mara said, charging his tormentor, throwing him across a desk and beginning to strangle him before he was pulled off. "Don't fuck around with my family."

"Hey, what's your problem?" Tomasulo said. "It's just a game."

"No it's not. It's my fucking family!" Mara yelled.

Someone had to make a play. Anyone. In the name of Mara. In the name of Rote. In the name of L. T. In the name of Simms. Give us just one play. Just one play that will live forever. . . .

Night falls in Tampa. It is January 1991, the time of the first Gulf War, but the Super Bowl must be played. The field is lit bright. Real green grass. Damp with the evening dew. Gaudy red-painted end zones, the stadium shamelessly tarted up for Super Bowl XXV. Photographers ring the field.

The Giants are trailing Buffalo by two. But they must come out here at the start of the second half and make a statement. They must inflict damage, take a bite. No more first-half ass-sniffing. The second half is about killing intentions and the infliction of mortal wounds.

With that in mind, No. 15 lopes in from the sideline toward the huddle. This is Jeff Hostetler, the quarterback of the New York Giants. The narrow-jawed Appalachian with the mustache and gloomy eyes. Who looks like he should be wearing a coonskin hat, not a football helmet.

The Giants' first play, Hostetler rolls right, barely avoids Buffalo linebacker Cornelius Bennett before bouncing a horrendous pass into the dirt that almost gets intercepted. Bennett blows the play up. Just destroys it. Basically rips the first page out of the Giants' second-half playbook, crumples it up and swallows it with wide, taunting eyes.

This being the Giants' very first statement about their intentions in the second half of Super Bowl XXV, you have to infer they lack what they need to win: execution, intelligence, imagination, better athletes. Pitiful. The assumption has to be that the Giants are going three-and-out and not merely back to the sideline but straight to the airport and home. How many teams that took the field to open the second half and went three-and-out on their first drive went on to win that Super Bowl? My guess is zero.

Then it gets worse. Offensive lineman Bob Kratch false-starts. You watch him go up to the line on the following play and carefully screw his cleats into the turf with the thoughtful frown of a smithy and you realize what Kratch and the whole team is thinking: Stop fucking up.

Which is when Hostetler rolls left, intelligently away from Bennett, and hits Dave Meggett on a screen. Meggett, no more than a sprite, spurts to the 27. The next play, Hoss dumps it over the middle to Meggett again, and Meggett somehow breaks the tackle and makes the first down. There is impetus.

Kratch's foot. That's what started it all. The way he plants his cleat after getting the procedure call. Like a strongman spitting on his palms before lifting a great weight. This is going to involve stick-to-itiveness, his small gesture implies. He understands that. They all understand that. It is a statement of purpose. It foretells what is about to transpire.

You part a beaded curtain to peek in at your sleeping kid. The kid has just turned fourteen. She knows nothing of what soaks your pajama collar at 3 A.M. and awakens you. Her main concern is Crazy Hair Day at school, how mean the popular girls are and the distributive function in algebra.

You are old enough to have begun forgetting how old you are and that she is just fourteen. Yet she's under similar stress—she is straining as hard forward as you are backward. You are opposing parentheses.

At her age, you had glasses, pimples, a slack jaw, a retainer and a pompadour you cemented into place using a green goo of epoxyesque strength labeled "Stay Neat."

Now? The forms, the bills, the applications, the sign-ups, the donations, the reservations and the contributions. The car needs an inspection sticker. Your Gibson J-45 acoustic needs new frets. You're wringing the last drops of equity out of your home the way a desert wanderer squeezes water from a moleskin pouch. Your health insurance is going to run out in another couple quarters. You don't remember any of your PIN numbers.

No, it's not that. That's just a smoke screen. Why're you up? You're haunted by the sight of Tiki coming off the field. Haunted by how awful it was. You can do all the right things, prepare all the right ways, but you are powerless. Tiki ducking away so unceremoniously. So thwarted.

Something rattles inside just to think of that word. *Thwarted.* The way you give something a shake to see if there's anything left inside. The same rattle you feel in your gut if you think that the best may no longer be before you. That rattle when the latest stone you've skimmed out across the waves splashes its last and finally sinks. You'd like it to stop rattling. You want Tiki Barber to show you how to "shut it down." That's the wonderful euphemism the baseball pitcher Roger Clemens used when he talked about pitching no more. He talked about "shutting it down." As if you weren't some ordinary person stumbling toward a fixed-income retirement and leaking heart valves, but a giant furnace, a nuclear reactor burning with the unstoppable energy of the sun itself, allowing a couple graphite rods to be adjusted a couple centimeters. Shutting it down.

Show me how to shut it down, Tiki.

"I want to go out a winner," Tiki says, "but you can't script life. You can't write the book before it happens."

"Third-and-one," Super Bowl announcer Al Michaels picks up as the Giants snap the ball, "Anderson again . . . and

Anderson into Buffalo territory . . . and Anderson all the way to the thirty-yard line . . . ."

You have to love the way O. J. Anderson ends the run with a whisker-jolting uppercut to the onrushing Buffalo defensive back, Mark Kelso.

Frank Gifford, with the announcing crew, can hardly contain himself. He's talking with a little lockjaw, as if the strap from his old Giants helmet was digging into his chin. Frank wants to suit up and get out there. Something's afoot. And here it comes, Michaels saying: "The flea-sized Meggett skids around the right side, first down . . . Flag down. . . ."

It's the Bavaro holding penalty against Cornelius Bennett. Hostetler fades to pass on the next play. He glances downfield, then squirts straight ahead out of the pocket, but is tweezered and barely gets across the line of scrimmage. The ball is on the Buffalo 32. It's third-and-thirteen, and they are too far away for a field goal.

It's still early in the game, but here's the pivotal moment, like the best cut on a great album:

Michaels says, "Third-and-13 . . . Hostetler throwing . . . caught by Ingram. . . ."

Ingram comes down with the pass a hair outside the 26. He is six yards short of the first down. He is surrounded on three sides by snorting Bills defenders. He has no chance. Not a prayer. He's dead meat. Having made his own assault at the first-down yardage and gotten essentially nowhere on the previous play, Hostetler has fallen back on some hickory-smoked truism: that sometimes the greatest achievements, those that employ the thinking of many and the exertions of many more, may rise or fall on the stroke of a lone man's ax. Just put the ax in his hand.

And so, Hostetler tosses the ball to Ingram. Here. You do it.

Ingram uses his cross-field momentum to sweep back upfield and beyond his immediate defender, Kirby Jackson, and he outflanks him laterally. Which leaves him no closer than before, still at least six yards from the first down. Returning to the job at hand, Ingram cuts to his left, downfield, to gain those six vital yards, as Buffalo linebacker Shane Conlan missiles at him. Ingram plants his right foot on the 25-yard line, stops dead and somehow wheels clockwise and back around. Conlan can't downshift fast enough. Passing by, a casualty of his own momentum, he sticks out his right arm and manages to collar Ingram.

But Ingram ducks, and the linebacker's own misdirected mass does Ingram's work for him—Conlan's right arm slips up and over Ingram's neck and off; Ingram has shrugged Conlan aside. He is now five yards from the first down, as three Buffalo defenders gobble up ground toward him from behind.

Ingram looks up from the spin to see Mark Kelso bearing in low and not two yards off. Kelso, jawbone still reverberating from O. J.'s right uppercut a few plays earlier, the bouquet of the revenge he is about to savor already preoccupying him, is prematurely absent self-restraint. Instantly, Ingram jukes left and Kelso bites, dropping to a knee and snatching at air as Ingram hops right, untouched, leaving Kelso behind. From this frying pan, Ingram leaps directly into the waiting arms of yet another defender.

Ingram employs the same plant-and-spin move, twirling clockwise once more to wrest himself away, even as Conlan, who'd picked himself up from the dust, moves in for yet another clean kill shot. There are five Bills in hot pursuit within two or three yards of Ingram and he is still three yards short.

He's got to make that first down.

At the 21, a fifth Bills player drives savagely into Ingram's left hip. But Ingram is already turning away off his left leg to cushion the blow. He seems almost to use the force to help corkscrew him around clockwise for yet the third time.

Conlan now takes his second shot. Only this time Ingram's already into his third whirl. Conlan misses again, this time to the other side. He clubs at Ingram with his left arm, but again fails to bring him down.

Somehow Ingram manages to complete his spin, planting his right cleat down on the 21. There are two guys clawing at him and six guys after him, but the important thing is, Ingram's right leg's free.

Essentially stopped, and hobbled on one leg, Ingram refuses to go down. He takes one more hop to complete his spin and calibrate his balance. The hop shows what kind of wits he has about him in the midst of this detonating physical chaos. And with what sort of grave athletic instinct he is able at this last-second moment to assess the situation and the yardage he needs, and what he has to do to get it, to plant and gather himself for the one, final, great surge of strength required. Ingram launches himself, men swirling, slamming, piling and rolling angrily all around him. Past the 20 . . . past the 19. First down.

"Wuh," is all TV announcer Dan Dierdorf can manage, he is so dumbfounded by what Ingram has just done. The moment dilates, glinting with bravery.

"Every now and then in a football play—in a game, rather—

you can look back to a play and it might set the tone for everything that happens after that. If the Giants win this game they may look back to this catch and run by Ingram," Dierdorf says.

And you appreciate him forever for zeroing in on exactly what this is from the very first. Every football drive is a statement, sometimes a whole story. And Dierdorf, with scholarly acumen, glimpses the text and knows what he's reading, which is something of durable merit, a classic. And keeps coming back to the grinding nature of the drive. How much it will wear out a defense.

Then it's Anderson up the middle and soon enough third-and-4 from the 12, the fourth such make-or-break crescendo of this symphonic drive. If they make this first down, there is no doubt they will score a touchdown. You don't grind out four firsts on a drive and not come away with six. But if they have to settle for three—if, after all they've done, they fail on this single play—then Buffalo has bent but not broken. There would be honor salvaged in having ultimately stood their ground. And the Giants would only lead by an insignificant one point.

Of the fourteen plays on this 9-minute, 29-second drive you rank the next as number 5. Ingram's number 1, of course. Number 2 would be O. J.'s run and uppercut to Kelso. Number 3 would have to be the upcoming touchdown itself. And number 4, by a hair, give to Meggett's third-and-7 dump pass catch-and-run conversion, as he broke tackles to make the necessary yardage.

But this is close. Third down again, remember. Hostetler rolls left this time. Tight end Howard Cross does a tremendous job of getting into Bruce Smith and selling the block, but then he expertly clears Smith and steams to the left flat. Smith rushes terrifyingly at Hostetler. He takes a monstrous leap into the air.

But Hostetler gets a soft pass away, lofting it perfectly over Smith to Cross, who has reappeared in the flat. Cross takes the pass and barrels out of bounds. First down at the three. The same play they ran the other way, and that was almost intercepted by Cornelius Bennett, the very first snap of the half. Nine minutes later it has all but put paid to the matter. But as deft as Hostetler's pass was, and as good as it had to be, give Cross the lion's share of the credit.

Dierdorf is all over the matter as Anderson plunges to the one. Providing that verbal musical score to the event that great announcers can do to fix the moment.

"This is the kind of drive that makes football coaches just light up with glee, or chew their gum even faster than normal [camera on Bills coach Marv Levy manically masticating on the sideline]. This is a tremendous drive by the New York Giants. This is a championship drive. . . . This is a Super Bowl drive."

And then it's handoff, Anderson, end zone. An explosion of rejoicing.

"That was one of the great drives in Super Bowl history," Dierdorf says. "That was physical domination."

Stop. Reverse. Play.

"This is a championship drive. . . . This is a Super Bowl drive. . . ."

Stop. Reverse. Play.

"This is a championship drive. . . . This is a Super Bowl drive. . . ."

Stop. Reverse. Pl—

"Are you okay?"

My wife is standing in the doorway to the den. She's not so much concerned as curious. "Curious" is her favorite word. She has always been very curious about my behavior, although not, I think, in the most innocent way, and, lately, she's gotten phenomenally curious about my behavior. The mutterings. The sighs. The clucking. The tsk-tsk. The RLS.

"It's three o'clock in the morning," she says. "You're watching a tape of an old football game?"

She's about to leave me sitting there in the dark when I say:

"Do you know how many plays there have been in all the Giants games ever played?"

"You know, I'm actually starting to feel sorry for you."

"Roughly, I would say, a hundred thirty, a hundred forty, a hundred fifty thousand. Over eighty years."

"I'm going back to sleep."

"I'm watching the single greatest play of all time."

"If I were you, I'd be watching pornography."

"I'm just telling you the guy's name. Mark Ingram. He should get a presidential pardon. Bush should sign the papers."

"Why does he need a pardon? He's in jail?"

"Convicted for drug money. I think the charge for grand theft auto and bank fraud were dropped. And he's a deadbeat dad. But he made that play."

"And now he's your hero. Oh, and speaking of deadbeat dad . . . Newmark sent over some new page we have to sign for the will. We have to get it notarized."

"I can have more than one hero, you know."

"Tiki's going to the podium."

"Tiki's going to the podium."

The flood of journalistic protoplasm smashes against the narrow locker doorway and spumes across a corridor into another room where Barber steps onto a raised platform and faces a battery of lights and cameras and microphones and reporters worthy of a visiting foreign minister. He accepts questions regarding the things he'd been doing in the last couple of hours before he went into the shower, came out and got dressed.

Here is what he did: He made plays. He got them into the playoffs.

In the last regular-season game of his career he ran for three touchdowns on runs of 16, 52, and 55 yards. He ran for 237 yards, a franchise record. And one 33-yard burst was called back for a holding call on center Shaun O'Hara.

He had been called a quitter. He had been called a distraction, and had the Giants not made the playoffs, his mid-season announcement that he was retiring would have been seen as an incontrovertible factor in the team's poor showing. Instead, when it was said and done, all this storied performance lacked was Grantland Rice writing about it from the press box.

On Thursday, after finishing practice and before traveling to Washington for the game, Tiki walked out of the Giants

Stadium tunnel for the last time. He said he actually felt better at this point this season than last. But he felt there were things he could no longer do, although he could not be specific.

"Maybe it's a cut, maybe it's a tackle that I break on a play, I just don't know. I can't pinpoint one thing. I can't say, 'Oh, this play against this one team I shoulda done this.' All I know is, today, I feel pretty decent. But after the game, on Monday, I won't feel that way and it'll take three or four days to come back from because that's the nature of this beast. When you're twenty-two it takes two days, and when you're thirty-one it takes four or five. I don't want it to take seven."

Late in the Redskins game, the Giants' defense had allowed its opponents so many opportunities to flood the stadium with "Hail to the Redskins" that if you heard that song one more time and had to watch those clowns running back and forth in the end zone waving those huge flags in celebration, you'd plunge your plastic cafeteria fork into someone's neck, maybe your own. Kevin Gilbride (the newly installed play caller) called Barber's number on five out of six straight plays. On the last of which, Barber nudged O'Hara into a block, downshifted for a split second to watch the linemen crash and topple like falling timber supports in a collapsing mine, planted his right foot and cut off it, then tore himself free of clutching defenders and briefly disappeared in the smoke of the struggle before suddenly emerging and running for a 50-yard touchdown.

As Dan Dierdorf would say, "Wuh."

"I knew in his last regular-season game he would make some kind of record," Shaun O'Hara had said in the Giants' locker room, "and that's what he did. He carried us to a win. This is what he does. This is Tiki Barber."

"Outstanding" is the word Coughlin uses to describe Tiki's game. If his tone got any more restrained, he'd be a casket salesman. Maybe he's still smarting from the words he and Tiki reportedly had behind closed doors in Jacksonville. "He just was not going down. On more than one of those runs he had people on his shoulders and on his back and his legs and he just kept right on going."

"Tiki had a fabulous game," Eli says. "The offensive line made some holes and he made a lot of guys miss, so . . . when we needed to make big plays we were making them. It was a great win today and a full team victory."

"Given the stakes and what was necessary for us, this game was right up there for me," Tiki tells the reporters who jam into the interview room. "I know what my job is and I do it very well, and when you get someone like Jim Finn listening when I tell him to stay on his path . . . Chris Snee and Dave Diehl making holes to allow me to run for touchdowns, big things happen."

He is asked what he said to Giants fullback Jim Finn when coming off the field early in the game, and Tiki, with his big equable smile, answers, "We had a draw play and Finny chased his linebacker instead of staying on his course and I came off the field and I told him, 'Hey, that was a touchdown if you stayed on your course,' and I said we have to run the same play and I told Kevin [Gilbride] and he called that play again and Finny stayed on his course and we had fifty-yard touchdown."

Some of the reporters ask if it's true he hasn't been taking his playbook home the last couple weeks. They make it sound as if Tiki has been having unprotected sex.

"Unless you've walked miles in my shoes and done all the things I've done, you can't understand what it takes for me to get myself ready for a football game. I've always said, judge me by what happens on the field. I have two kids at home," Tiki says, "so I leave my work at the stadium and that's where I prepare and that's worked for me. I've been playing this game an awful long time and I know when I get an opportunity to do my job that I'm awful damn good."

This doesn't seem to be a satisfactory answer for some. They demand to know if Tiki will take his playbook home with him this week, now that they're in the playoffs against Philadelphia. Tiki doesn't respond too much to that, although I felt like interjecting, "Did you just watch the game? Did you not just see the man run for two-fifty and change and three scores? Do you really need to know if he's going to bring his stupid fucking playbook home with him this week like a good boy?"

In the narrow corridor outside the interview room, Tiki exchanges a kiss with his wife, Ginny. The motors on the team buses whine and the brakes huff. They are breaking down the set. The duffels are being thrown together. The Giants have chartered a train for their return to the city, a quaint echo of earlier decades, but still there is this clamor in the air. FedEx Field is throbbing, as if the stadium ramps and walls are beginning to suck wind and mutter, "Okay, enough already, Tiki, you're wearin' me out." There is still this much of what Tiki brought with him whirling around and unspent.

The staccato beeping of a golf cart backing up claps off the walls. Tiki shakes a few more hands and heads with the golf cart through the crowd and back out onto the now-deserted stadium field. A mist, a blanket of evaporated human effort, clings to the grass parting before the wheels as the golf cart carrying precious cargo Tiki glides the man to one last station. His "performance" isn't over.

Out in the rolling Maryland countryside, traffic is jammed up for miles, doing loop-de-loops on the Beltway, choked with fans and those who've been forced way off course by security closures for President Gerald Ford's funeral ceremonies in the capital. And all those hundreds of thousands of cars tires are wobbling still from the tremors in the ground touched off by Tiki Barber's feet.

It's Saturday night and everyone wants to get home and run under the blankets, a natural human, shelter-seeking reaction to the extraordinary (and I don't mean Gerald Ford's funeral). I think of the cabdriver who brought me to the stadium, a Giants fan who called in his dinner order and was hoping to drop me off and pick it up, and I hope he's gotten home and enjoyed his chicken. He'd told me he wouldn't watch the game on TV and wouldn't watch the nightly news because he preferred learning about the game by looking at the headline in the *Washington Post* on his doorstep the next morning. I recall fondly his devotion to the unique graphic snap of a morning newspaper headline, and I envy the wonderful feeling he'll have, coffee cup in hand, when he picks up the *Post* tomorrow.

No one could possibly want to get home more than the postgame TV crew for the NFL Network. It's midnight, the stadium is empty, the maintenance crews are breaking it down, rolling up hoses and wiring, but these guys—Rich Eisen, Steve Mariucci, and Marshall Faulk—have to remain on the field, tired and chilled to the bone yet performance-ready behind their cheap phony "desks" to do a postgame sigmoidoscopy.

Tiki gets hooked up to talk about what he just did. But the words are meaningless compared with the deed. Perhaps they are diminished by the queer juxtaposition of having a guy on a panel all dressed in his suit talk about the great things he did a few minutes ago on the field right here when he wasn't wearing the suit and sitting at a desk. Anyway, it seems inherently less interesting. But Tiki, of course, goes with the performance. He understands the acting part of what he does very well. He is a running, darting content provider.

When the interview's over and the show wraps, the crew can begin lifting the fake desks and putting them in a truck. Mariucci undoes his microphone, drops it off with the sound guy and turns to go. The former coach of the Lions and, of course, the 49ers has dark circles under his eyes. I'm not sure if he's bored or whether his suddenly distracted look is simply that of a performer who's come off camera and is shedding all of that being focused-on. But either way, it's late and he's got somewhere else to be and he is certainly not disposed to be badgered.

"Whaddya think, Mooch? Huh? Was that somethin'? Was that something else? Huh, Coach? Mooch? Huh? 'Scuse me, Coach. Did you see Tiki? Huh, Mooch? Have y'ever seen any better performance than that? Huh?"

Mariucci half turns. He looks confused. The tone of the way he's being hectored has led him to expect he'll come face-to-face with a boy. But there can't be any boys here—it's way past everyone's bedtime.

The NFL Network crew has begun rolling up cable and breaking down the phony desks. The golf cart draws up to Tiki Barber. It will get him comfortably and swiftly across the field and back onto the bus to the train station and home.

Tiki Barber is now dressed *and* interviewed. And good to go. He leaves FedEx Field and the Redskins insignia at its center—that brave in profile, with the high forehead and feathers descending from his hair—only now it's pockmarked by clumps of gouged-aside sod. Tonight, Tiki Barber has chewed it up. Torn it to bits. Beaten it to a pulp. Scalped it. I walk out to the middle of the field and take a picture of it on my cell phone.

"Huh, Coach? Huh, Mooch! Was that good? Tell me that wasn't the best you ever saw. Huh? Huh, Coach? I know you coached some great ones. But to get into the playoffs like that? Three touchdowns? Huh, Mooch?"

Chapter 9

The Grim Scalper

You understand this is just the first screening for the Rise and Shine Restless Leg Syndrome Study, sir? If you progress and are accepted into the program, there would be another, lengthier screening. If you are included in the study, you would be required to take certain medications that have not yet been approved for this use by the United States Food and Drug Administration."

"I understand," I mumble into the phone.

"Now I'm going to ask you a few questions and our nurses will look it over and if they decide you should be part of the study, you might have to travel to a site near your address. The closest one is in Northridge. Would that be okay? We provide you with fifty dollars in travel expenses. I'm sorry, but with gas prices this high, that's not very—"

The only man ever to make the Pro Bowl on offense and defense, Frank Gifford.
NEIL LEIFER

"It's no problem. Money's no object. I just want a good night's sleep."

"And you might have to make yourself available for a series of ten weekly outpatient visits over twelve weeks, some of them lasting two and a half hours, at least four times in ten days if you are part of the study. Would that be okay?"

"Would I have to go to sleep in a lab or something?"

"No."

"Too bad."

"This is a double-blind study. We will be asking all participants to record a daily sleep-log entry on a Palm Pilot which we give you and then you upload onto a dedicated Web site. We will ask you such questions as the quality of your sleep, whether you had any exercise . . . how many meals you had and what you ate that day . . . your caffeine intake . . . that sort of thing. And whether you experience any PLM."

"What's PLM?"

"Periodic Leg Movements. At night. Now, can you describe your symptoms, sir?"

"I can't stop my legs. They're all creepy and crawly. They won't stay still. At night, I could be sitting down, or later, in bed, trying to go to sleep. I'm driving my wife crazy. My legs just keep twitching. I can't control it."

"Okay, and how often do you experience these symptoms? Would you say, three times a month? Once a week? Three times a week?"

"More. My hips aren't in the best shape. You don't suppose that could be it, do you?"

"That's why we're running the Rise and Shine Restless

Leg Syndrome Study, sir. Now, how long have you had these symptoms?"

"At least since opening day."

"Excuse me?"

"Six, seven months. I'm not sure exactly, but that's when it really started driving my wife crazy. Let me ask you something—is it possible I could get RLS from a football team?"

"Another nurse will do an evaluation, sir—"

"Because I think that's what it very well might be. Don't you see? Every time something goes good, something goes bad. Every time they could win, they don't win, and when you don't think they will, maybe they will. Do you see what I'm saying? They jerk you around. Back and forth. Back and forth. Like a twitch."

"I'm going to read a list of diseases and conditions to you, sir. If you have or have ever had any of them, just tell me 'yes' or 'stop.' Arteriosclerosis . . . dysentery . . . head trauma . . . epilepsy—"

"Giants."

"Sir?"

"That's my disease. It's the football team. That's what I'm trying to tell you."

"Who were you talking to on the phone before, Dad? What was all that about twitching?"

My daughter and I are sitting in our favorite restaurant in L.A. a week after New Year's. We flew back to Santa Monica yesterday. My wife is in Vermont doing a two-week stint of graduate work for her low-residency program. It comes at a great time for her. Drawing an inside straight: two weeks away from two tweens: her daughter and her husband.

I'm happy to have this time alone with Chloe. At this moment, for this short while, watching her is like seeing a shimmer in a glass of water, like seeing time itself. I want everything to be good for her. I want sunshine to flood her memories. I want her to be able to count on her dad. To be able to go out—just her and her dad—and have a nice dinner together. Which is exactly what we're doing tonight at Takao in Brentwood. Her favorite.

"The halibut sashimi with peppercorns?"

"Go for it," I say.

"Whitefish new style with truffles, Dad?"

"Live it up," I say.

"Tuna tartare, or is that too expensive? I mean . . . what we're getting is pretty expensive already, Dad."

"Get anything you want."

I've timed it perfectly. I wait for the hot hand towels. I figure that's the best time. The waitress approaches, clacking a pair of tongs.

"Listen, I know we only just got back from New York yesterday and your mom is all the way across the country," I say to my daughter, glancing up nervously to gauge her reaction, "but I have to go away for a couple days."

"What? You're leaving?"

"Yeah. Sorry."

"But why? Who'll I stay with?"

The hand towel doesn't appear to be soothing her very much. She's in middle school and life is a six-inch-wide balance beam when you're that age. You can never set your feet.

Who's sitting with whom at lunch? Who got True Religion jeans? Who goes to the Century City Mall and who goes to the Promenade in Santa Monica? How many friends do you have on your MySpace page? And have you been dropped out of someone's top eight? It's more fraught than my life is, for sure.

"I spoke with Grandma, and she said you could stay with her Saturday night and Sunday."

"Is this for the stupid Giants? The game is *this* Sunday? Jeez."

She dumps her washcloth onto the little wooden rack. For her, it is as lacking in warmth as I am. A comfort no longer. I remind myself to chamber a dessert visit down the block to Cold Stone if more ammo is needed in this standoff over my deserting her to go back East.

"I told you they'd win, didn't I? Remember when you called me in Seattle?"

She laughs. Her hysterical reaction at halftime during that game has become a joke between us. It's good that she can laugh at herself. This ought to be a natural stage of human development, somewhere on the list that starts way back with rolling over in the crib, but so many people never learn to kick off their shoes. The cleat rule.

"See, and here they are, in the playoffs. I can't miss that."

"But I thought they already played Philadelphia."

"During the regular season. They beat Philadelphia and then they lost at home."

"Oh, yeah . . . How could they lose at home?"

I resist going Stephen Mara on her and say, "You know what Eli Manning said in the locker room after the game against Washington?"

"No," she says. "What'd Eli say?"

"He said, 'We're in the playoffs and that's all you can ask for. We gotta figure out ways to keep winnin' games and play smart. Hopefully we can make some plays and keep it goin' and give it a shot next week.' "

"What's that mean?"

"It means it's a brand-new season. It's like a do-over. Once you're in the playoffs, it doesn't matter what your record was. You have a chance to win the Super Bowl.

"What was the Giants' record?"

"Eight and eight. But Pittsburgh won the Super Bowl last year and they were a wild-card team. Y'know what Tiki told me? He said, 'The NFL is all about momentum and confidence.'

"And now they have momentum. They already won in Philadelphia earlier in the year. Tiki said they're having a resurgence. You don't want me to miss that, do you?"

"But I have a math test on Monday. If you're not here, who's going to help me study? I can't study math with Grandma."

"I'll help you before I leave."

"I hate graphing things. Xy axis . . . two x plus three times negative four x minus nine—who's gonna help me study that? Plus I lost my compass, and so you have to buy me a new one in case I need it for the test."

"I'll get you ten compasses," I say.

"You love the Giants," my daughter says, "more than you love me."

I used to have a cheap metal compass in my school kit for math class. I'm sure you did, too. I kept it inside a plastic sleeve, yellow on one side and clear on the other.

The most important use I had for it wasn't geometry tests, though. Rather, it was drawing a circle with a radius of seventy-five miles on the map of New York I got down from the tool cabinet over the refrigerator one day when I was thirteen or fourteen.

I slid my compass out of its plastic sleeve and unfolded the map on the Formica kitchen table, while my mother was heating up some fish sticks. I figured out the map key and then stuck the point into where Yankee Stadium was in the Bronx and swung the pencil in a circle. The arc crossed Connecticut. Crossed the Long Island Sound. And then passed across Long Island. Way out near the tip. This was past Babylon. Past Jones Beach, which was as far east as I'd ever gone. I would somehow have to get somewhere way beyond where I'd ever been before to watch a crucial, late-season Giants-Steelers game next Sunday. And I had to convince someone to drive me there. I was battling the dreaded curse of the broadcast blackout.

My brother was the likeliest recruit. He had just gotten his license, and, to my mind, the whole point of getting a driver's license—or for the entire automotive industry, for that matter; in fact, the only good that ever came out of the internal combustion engine—was exactly so you could drive seventy-five miles to watch the Giants game.

"Don't be ridiculous," he said when asked. "They show the game in a bar. You have to be eighteen. They'll take one look at you and laugh you out of the joint."

Wednesday night before the Giants-Steelers game that week, I was standing on a raised stool staring at a daunting sight: me, trying on new pants, in a three-way mirror.

It was Landau Ltd., a new clothing store on the South

Shore opened by my friend Bruce's parents, who lived right across the backyard fence.

"All the kids want them tapered to nine or ten," Bruce's mom, Rose, said, bending beside me with a yellow tape measure draped around her neck. She was a large, kindhearted woman who called what I had just uneasily waddled out of the dressing room wearing "a pant."

While my mother debated how much of a hoodlum she'd let her thirteen-year-old son with horn-rims walk around looking like, I engaged Jack Landau. I'd heard from Bruce that Jack had mused about traveling beyond the blackout limit to watch a game recently.

"Big game on Sunday, huh, Mr. Landau? The Steelers."

Jack looked sideways at me. I was too young to know that when a man spends all his working hours in the company of his wife, you could ask him if he wanted to drive two hours each way to watch bulls being castrated, and he'd begin digging for his car keys.

"Where're they playing?" Jack asked, watching Rose measure the pant hem. He lingered because there were no other customers, a sign to me that the store's popularity was waning.

I felt guilty embarking on my plan, making prey out of Bruce's family. But I had no choice, since my brother had refused.

"Yankee Stadium."

"How wide should he have the pant cuff, Phyllis?" Rose asked from the floor. I glanced again at myself in the three-way mirror. I looked the opposite of how Frank Gifford looked in those Van Heusen shirt and Vitalis ads. He looked like a man, a heroic god. So did Kyle Rote. They could wear ten layers of clothes, all tucked in, and still look thin.

"If they don't beat the Steelers, they're in trouble," I said.

"They're blacked out?"

"Of course. And they're sold out."

"Sold out?"

"They always are. So it's not like you could buy a ticket even if you wanted. There are no seats."

"They black it out even if they're sold out?" Jack asked.

I realized that somehow wasn't a crucial enough fact for Jack Landau to make the central organizing principle of his existence the way I had. My world was basically divided into weeks when I could look forward to watching the Giants in an away game on Sunday, and weeks when I couldn't, when they were at home and all that glory was going down right under my nose, or, at least, within seventy-five miles of it.

"You say it's a big game, huh?" Jack Landau asked. He had almost gelatinous reddish hair that he swept back, and a nose so pudgy it crinkled up his eyes.

"Biggest game of the season. Boy, wouldn't you love to see it? When I grow up, I'm going to buy a house exactly seventy-five miles from Yankee Stadium so I get to watch every game."

"Where do you think you're going?" my brother asked me a few days later when he found me as I donned what my mother called my "lumber jacket" by the front closet and reached to pull from the top shelf the red hat with the fold-down earmuffs.

"To the Giants game," I said, trying to whistle nonchalantly, although I had never been able to whistle. "Jack Landau's driving me and Brucie out on the Island. Past the blackout."

"Where? To a bar? They'll never let you in, runt."

"I'll let you know how it turns out," I said.

As protection against being thrown out of the bar for being too young, I lifted my brother's driver's license. I understood there was something wrong about this, but the thought that he might drive somewhere and for whatever reason get stopped by the cops and find himself without a license and wind up in jail because of what I'd done and wind up having his ass tanned by my dad somehow didn't deter me. Big brothers will force little ones to lengths beyond their surmise.

The ID wasn't a problem, though, as it turned out. Somewhere out in Center Moriches or Hauppauge or Westhampton or Riverhead, Jack pulled into a parking lot next to some docks by the bay and walked into where the Rheingold sign was lit up a fluorescent pink, and made sure the coast was clear.

There was hardly anyone inside and the bartender didn't object to our sitting at a table in the corner. Men in red hunting caps sipped coffee or drank beer and not a single cheer emerged from their throats. Jack bought us an order of fries to share and a Coke each and made it clear that had to last the whole game, but I didn't care.

My plan and its execution were impeccable, as few things were at that age. The only problem, it turned out, was I couldn't see the game.

It was on TV. But this wasn't one of those modern sports bars with plasma screens. This joint had one TV with a set of brown rabbit ears. No matter which way the owner aimed them, all you could see was a blizzard of morphing ghosts and shadows and spots and speckles. What you might call an actual picture never really settled in. Maybe all you saw was two fat guys at the bar reenacting the game. This was what I'd risked my neck and finagled my way seventy-five miles for.

But I didn't mind. Even though I couldn't tell what was going on, enough was revealed simply by being in its presence for the game to enter into my limbic system as much as any you might see clearly, even at Yankee Stadium. I knew their names—Robustelli, Katcavage, Patton, Tunnell, Huff, Livingston et al., pounded at again and again by John Henry Johnson and Buddy Dial and the rest of the Steelers, who brought hell every time they played. And it all inevitably swirled toward the dark moments late in the game when something bitterly important was on the line and in danger of being lost.

All I could make out was that they were deep in their own territory and that it was third down and long. The rest was dots and cracks and hisses and pops that composed somehow for only an instant into the slender, triple-formed shadow of No. 16, Frank Gifford, reaching back low and to his right and somehow collaring a desperate pass, before it again atomized into the ether.

Gifford had somehow made a catch. The Giants had somehow won.

The alarm goes off at three A.M. on Sunday morning, January 7. It's actually a relief to get out bed and stop twitching. The bad thing about waking up in the dark is that there's no fighting the fact that you are going to have to turn a light on and look at yourself in the mirror in sudden, full illumination. This is like going from 0 to 60 in a tenth of a second straight into a brick wall. After a few moments of blinking and rubbing, you stand there thinking surely your eyesight isn't done adjusting. Surely if you rub a little harder and get all that sleep out of your eyes and come into sharper focus, you won't actually look this ready for a morgue slab.

I bet the Giants slept better than me. They're probably still asleep in their hotel in Philadelphia. I asked Kiwanuka once how he slept knowing that the fate of the team had fallen on his shoulders like a ton of bricks.

"I don't know about a ton of bricks," he protested.

"All right, how about a pound of bricks," I said. "An ounce of bricks . . . ? A feather . . . ?"

Kiwanuka said he slept just fine.

But look at me. Is that candle wax dripping off my face, or is that my neck? And here's something else I can make out: that reddened topography on my chin. I haven't seen one of these in years—but there's no mistaking. It's a zit. A little red volcano.

This is great. I crossed Long Island with zits to see them forty-five years ago, and I'm crossing the continent with zits to see them today. Unfortunately, the twenty-four-hour Zit Maintenance and Repair Shop I used to run back in the day is long since boarded up and deserted. Has been for years. A good thing, too. They're perilous. One time—just one time in my entire life—I sterilized a pin with a match and went at one. A few days later I went blind in my right eye. Optic neuritis. It was highly entertaining to peer into a mirror and watch one of your eyeballs roll up milky white into your skull. The first doctor I saw decided I had an inoperable brain tumor and threw me out of his office in a manner that would have disturbed Hippocrates almost as much as it did me. The second doctor I consulted said it was optic neuritis and wondered how

I got it and to this day I've never told a soul it was undoubtedly the result of an infected needle I'd used on a stupid, fucking pimple, the sort of thing you're told never, ever to do.

On that long list of "don't ever do this" things, I really don't have that many check marks. The doctor gave me massive doses of cortisone and my sight returned. But, decades later, that cortisone was responsible for building up fat deposits that blocked blood from flowing through the one slender vein that carries it to your hip bone. And, as a result of that one not totally sterilized pinprick, I have bilateral osteo-necrosis. Standing for a long while, jumping, walking long distances on concrete—not fun. It's the same condition that forced Bo Jackson out of football.

Do any of the Giants look as roughed up as I do as the day of reckoning dawns on what could be the last game of the season? I haven't even played and I'm a physical wreck. Forget the sleep, the awful truth is that even having to do the flying two, three times a month, the way the players do, is as much as I can bear. My back is as bad as Luke Pettigout's. My hips are worse than Osi Umenyiora's. My knee as twisted as Amani Toomer's. My foot as tender as Michael Strahan's.

I try to console myself with a thought: At least I've made the PUP list, the acronym for Physically Unable to Play. Players who can't play are put on that list. And if *they* are physically unable and I am as well, then maybe we're all on the PUP list together, although, in my case, permanently.

I can think of only two words at three A.M. while horrifying myself in the mirror getting ready to fly across the country to watch the Giants in the first round of the 2006 playoffs, and they aren't "Big Blue," they are "horse's ass." That's what my father would have called me. A horse's ass. He would have assured me, no way in a million years would the Giants win this game.

I pad down the darkened hallway of our home. Below the cabinet that holds the furnace and the clean linens and towels is a small door to another cupboard that holds the artifacts of a five-decade-long sporting life coming down to its last few plays on an outdoor basketball court at John Adams Middle School on Saturday afternoons at 2 P.M.—rackets, my baseball gloves going back to junior high, a basketball, and a football.

The house is empty. Wife back East. Kid at grandma's. I haven't lost my family, of course, haven't technically forfeited them in my odyssey, yet I can't help realizing that this is the first time since the arrival of our child well more than a decade ago that we are split apart. Separate. The three of us each under a different roof. I am aware of being alone, not in some hotel or on some trip, but alone in my own home. I am aware of being without.

There is nothing else here but me. No distractions. No matters of school or acting class or social plans or errands or agendas to surround myself with as buffers.

"You are what you can't get rid of," Philip Roth wrote. Alone in the dark, what I can't get rid of is doubt. I'm not sure about the Giants. I realize that this doubt about the Giants is just the tell, that it is part of a drumbeat of bigger, inner doubts.

Tiki might be at the end of his run. What if I am, too? What if, next time you shake me, you don't hear anything in there? I think of the last TV show. *NCIS*. I'd written a script about a former Marine who fought on Iwo Jima. He believes he murdered a friend of his during the battle and has to be, in screenwriters' parlance, "gaslit" (the term derives from the

1944 Charles Boyer–Ingrid Bergman movie) into remembering he isn't guilty. Charles Durning played the role. I was overjoyed. I was knocked out by his performance. Take after take. Hour after hour. Dragging himself back and forth across the soundstage from the set to the door and out to his trailer. Time and time again.

I could have been fused to the video assist, the lighting, giving notes to the director or talking with Charlie. I could have given nitpicky notes to some of the other actors. But all I did for four hours was sit there and look at the floor and make sure Charlie didn't trip on the cables and wires when he was coming onto the set, because that's all that stood between us and something great (Charlie wound up being nominated for an Emmy). And now, in the dark, at home, I remind myself not to "trip on the cables" as I psych myself up for my job today.

I put the doubt behind me. I turn on the light in my daughter's bathroom. I find some Proactiv and go to work on my zit and take one last look in the mirror.

I must go. It's an attempt at personal redemption. My moment of shame came in Tampa for the Super Bowl against the Baltimore Ravens in 2000. The game fell during the local "mardi gras" celebration known as Gasparilla. It was a weeklong bacchanal with a football game thrown in. And while I was there, I did three things of which I'm not terribly proud.

Numbers one and two, combined in no particular order (which is pretty nearly how they did happen), are: Mons Venus. Scrambled eggs. Free T-shirt. Lynn Swann. Smelly socks. Breast. Pirate ship. Jackie Slater. Scrambled eggs. Free beer. Beads. Commissioner Paul Tagliabue. Nipples. Sponge fishing. Gilbert Roland. Parking garage. Fresh grapefruit.

Wallace Matthews of *Newsday*. Big package. Punch in the solar plexus. Free beer. *Maxim* party.

Number three was the worst, though. I scalped my Giants ticket. I'd gone to the Super Bowl with my friend Dave, and wherever we wandered on our beaded and besotted journey, a scalper named Dex seemed never to be far from our trouser cuffs. Always yapping at us about how much our Super Bowl tickets were worth. He worked the streets relentlessly.

Once I'd been aghast that a lifelong Giants fan, Fred Exley, could have a ticket and not go into the Rose Bowl to see his team play in Super Bowl XXI. But in Tampa I reached the point where I bailed on the Giants as Exley had. The crowd was so enormous and the party so continuous and crushing that there was pretty nearly no way to get to places that you couldn't walk to. Vehicular movement was next to impossible. We'd left our rental car in the hotel parking garage. And on the night we were supposed to attend a tennis event hosted by my former boss at *SPORT* magazine, the late Dick Schaap, the street onto which the only entrance to the parking garage emptied was hosting some sort of debauched Gasparilla parade. The line of cars trying to get out of the parking structure and onto the blocked-off street backed all the way up to the third floor, where we found our car, got in, turned on the motor, and prepared to go to the party. We backed up the car six inches. And that's as close as we got. There was no way to move. We pulled the car back in six inches and got out and proceeded to . . . Well, you can refer to the list above.

It's taken me years to realize that this first enactment of not going someplace led to the more regrettable reenactment wherein we scalped our tickets and didn't go to the Giants-Ravens Super Bowl.

Of course, we had also partied ourselves into such a coma that the game had become somewhat irrelevant. And so, late one night, we struck a deal with Dex, and I exchanged the prospect of Ray Lewis for a piece of my daughter's school tuition. I never went to the Super Bowl. I lied about it to people. Then I tried to sound clever about it. I tried to justify it. Like I did just now. It got me some cash for my kid's education. Moral justification.

I don't know if in the scale of things, scalping my Giants ticket is big or not very much at all. It's definitely unreported income, there's no doubt about that. Which is no trifle. But even if, or when, I write out a tax check, I'll remain remorseful not for turning my back on Uncle Sam, but for turning my back on the Giants. It's left me with a sour taste in my mouth that lingers to this day, to this early Sunday morning. When I made that exchange I turned into something I never thought I could or would become, the person I absolutely couldn't fathom when I looked at Fred Exley outside the Rose Bowl that afternoon in 1987: a man who'd lost his appetite.

Now, I have the chance to redeem myself by proving that I will never turn my back on the Giants again. The boy I was has enough appetite to help me do the nearly impossible: get up this early in the morning to fly across the country to Philadelphia and watch the Giants take their first step toward the Super Bowl.

MVP of the Giants' all-time Messiest Divorce Team, Michael Strahan. RICH KANE

Chapter 10

The Final Gun

The Eagles play in a jail. That's what Lincoln Financial Field is—a $512 million football stadium built around a hoosegow for locking up drunks and miscreants at the games. This makes the City of Brotherly Love unique among North America's great sports towns in that its state-of-the-art sports arena requires not only the maximum number of luxury boxes, but the maximum number of nonluxury boxes, as it were.

As you approach through potholed South Philly, the car window jumpily frames the asphalt wastes and people's blurred, scurrying backs, evoking the anonymous mayhem you get on the evening news of the violence in Baghdad. Ominous. The skies couldn't be bleaker. It's beginning to drizzle. I'm warned repeatedly not to linger around the stadium or to, for whatever reason, even under the threat of waterboarding, confess that I am a Giants partisan. Otherwise I will require hospitalization. Stupidly, I have neglected to bring my bulletproof vest to the game.

"The Linc" is hardly welcoming for the Giants players, either. They are spit upon, cursed at and have beer and garbage dumped on them. The team buses bringing them into the stadium are regularly accosted and soiled.

Earlier in the year, during the regular-season visit in September, Tiki looked out upon the sea of dancing middle fingers and epithet-hollering Eagles fans and decided he might prefer some slightly less obscenity-laced surroundings—like a TV studio, say—to work in. I'd bet the thought of never having to play in Philadelphia again pushed his decision to retire over the top.

I'm simply hoping they have my credential here. Half the time on the road and sometimes even at Giants Stadium, I get a credential—after doing all the requisite officials' foreskin rubbing to get it, mind you—only I show up and discover there's no credential. No pass under my name. I slide my driver's license to the person behind the window who doesn't see my name on his or her list. I say:

"Look at the driver's license. I'm from California. See?"

The person looks up from my license. They see. I'm a real person, and not just a sniffy asshole trying to talk my way past the gates by claiming a position of authority as the director of something (thanks to my surname, I regularly get mail addressed to my relatives art, gym, bank, and choir).

"Do you think I live in Santa Monica and I flew all the way across the country to (fill in the blank) (a) a pisspot like Philadelphia; (b) some Texas redneck hellhole like Dallas; (c) Hicktown, USA (aka Landover, Maryland), with the idea of sneaking my way into the game?"

"I don't see your name on the list, sir."

"Look at me closer. This isn't a phony ID. Do I look like I'm some sixteen-year-old trying to sneak into an R-rated movie? Like I'm running some scam here?"

"All I can tell you, sir, is that I don't have your name on the list."

"I was told it'd be on the list. I got up this morning in California. Understand? I got up this morning in Santa Monica and I came here. There's a palm tree across my alley."

For some reason, this is what usually gets them. I think it's this sudden appearance at the invariably icicle-encrusted Eastern Division stadium's will-call window of a tanned Californian with a palm tree out his window. The yarn this daft old man's spinning is just freakish and unusual enough to be true, they think. They motion over a twenty-year-old PR intern. And after I explain that I am following the Giants around and I got up this morning and instead of going to the Sunday Santa Monica Farmers' Market down by the beach, eating freshly made lemon and sugar crepes, listening to live music, and feasting my eyes on the hordes of magnificent, sleepy, sunlit women, so lately out of bed and dressed that your imagination is beckoned to imagine them before they were, I came here, to (a) or (b) or (c), the intern gets to issue the first executive order of his or her working life: Let this dumb bastard in.

Other than the credential, there are no other necessities for me to possess. In fact, I've brought along next to none. I am traveling light. I have only the green shoulder bag I carry to every Giants game. In various zippered compartments, this holds: Two legal pads. One reporter's notebook. Eight "buck" slips (movie studio note cards) for shows from *Hill Street Blues* to *Moonlighting* to *Arli$$*. Three No. 2 Berol Black Warrior pencils. Five pens. Sudafed. The 2006 New York Giants Information Guide. The "flip cards" (the laminated personnel charts with the lineups, vital stats and uni numbers) from the last few games. A pound of press releases ("Tonight's National Anthem will be sung by the Performing Arts Academy Vocal Ensemble of the Ocean County Vocational Technical School"). One broken Radio Shack microcassette recorder with six extra AA batteries and a small plastic bag full of microcassettes along with the operating instructions. A recently bought, brand-new digital recorder that worked once in a test run at home yesterday and better work now or all Radio Shack employees are dead meat. A felled forest's worth of accumulated Jet Blue boarding passes and printed out, e-mailed ticket confirmation and itinerary reminders. One pack of green Tic Tacs. One pack of orange Tic Tacs. A New York Giants Schedule. A Rolodex card from Landry's seafood house, 400 North Peters Street, New Orleans. Bills from the Clarion and the Fairfield Inn in Beltsville, Maryland.

I'm also toting my cell phone charger. A picture of my daughter and me dancing at her bat mitzvah. An airport newsstand package of Oreos. Two big packs of Juicy Fruit. A copy of James Agee's *A Death in the Family*. A box of Cracker Jacks. A piece of custom-made notepaper my daughter gave me. On one side is a message: "Daddy, I love you! You'll finish your book and it'll be great!! I promise! Xoxo Your daughter Chloe." Using a ruler, she'd drawn nine lines across the other side of the paper, and under a heading she'd written: "You can write your ideas here:"

I also have a folder of newspaper clippings I collect about the Giants in the green bag, including two recent ones I especially like by Dave Anderson: his instant classic, the salute to Tiki Barber, "Wave Goodbye to a True New York Giant," and "Empty Seat on Giants Bus to Philadelphia," about the sudden death of seventy-three-year-old Roy Posner, who collapsed while standing with the Giants on the New Carrollton, Maryland, platform waiting for the chartered train to take them back to Newark. He'd been one of the white-haired gentlemen standing almost beatifically along the locker room wall, his cheeks pink with admiration, as Tiki and the team got dressed after the game against Washington one week ago.

I read Anderson's Roy Posner column over and over. It seems to me that perhaps some tax had been exacted by Fate for Tiki's superhuman effort that night against the Redskins. Maybe it was just the terrible adrenal jolt the benign Posner experienced when he was pelted by lemons outside FedEx Field waiting to board the team bus that would ferry them to the train. Citrus, not lead, sure, but projected with the anarchic insanity of assassins. To have something so dark occur right on the platform at the moment of boarding your victory train for the triumphant return home with center Shaun O'Hara bent over him, pleading, "You've got to fight, Roy," can't help but raise speculation that you're cursed.

Posner's death is a reminder, a reiteration of the deaths of the team's two owner/patriarchs—Well Mara and Bob Tisch—in the past fourteen months. Individually no player has any explanation for the way things have gone this year, and I conclude that in ways no one is keen to recognize—these are grown-ups and professionals, after all, making millions of dollars at a job—the team is exactly what it says: mystified. Unmoored, the way one drifts uselessly in a fog for months, years even, following the death of a father or mother. There is no game film or practice drill to help you find your way out of the long shadows such deaths cast. Not a paper was touched in Wellington Mara's old office for ten months after he died. John wouldn't move in until opening day. The team is in the dumps, anxious, irritable, out of breath and appetite. The Giants aren't out of mourning.

Contrary to the reassurance I gave my daughter over sashimi the other night, and adding to the pervasive sense of gloom, the one idea I could scribble down on her sweet notepaper is this: No one really thinks the Giants can win this game. On the weekly pregame show, *Giants Online*, none of the panelists—beat reporters—think the Giants will beat Philadelphia.

This is both a testament to the objectivity of the reporters who regularly cover the team and simple logic. No sane person, having watched the first sixteen games the team played this year, sees a squad capable of rising to the occasion. Of meeting the challenge. Of making themselves winners. Of turning questions and doubts into statements and proofs.

Maybe a little magic can help. Before the game, the Giants' Hall of Fame middle linebacker Harry Carson gave his 1986 Super Bowl ring to Tiki Barber. Tiki passed it around among his teammates at the pregame supper. As if it were a nugget of gold handed around a boardinghouse table, circa 1850, for each lodger to examine in turn, as a way of inciting a yearning that would prompt each to retire to his room upstairs and come down shortly thereafter changed into buckskin and carrying a knapsack, determined to head out west to California and strike it rich.

"We knew what it took to win a Super Bowl," Carson told me. "We knew what it was going to require of ourselves. We had to learn to do the little things necessary to win. We checked our egos at the door so that we could be the best we could be. I didn't necessarily want to play in New York when I was drafted. But after I got here I learned about the history and the tradition of the team, of what happened in the fifties. You learn about it from the trainers who taped the ankles of Y. A. Tittle and Sam Huff and all those guys. My goal all along was that when I left the Giants I wanted to be remembered in the same way you thought about Robustelli and Huff and Tittle—you would mention Harry Carson. That was my only goal. To be mentioned in the same breath as those other players."

Maybe this evening in Philadelphia, when crunch time comes, "when the team is up against it," to use George Gipp's deathless phrase, one of the Giants' defenders will rise up the way Harry Carson did in Super Bowl XXI. The Broncos had first-and-goal on the Giants' one-yard line. On second and third downs Denver tried to push the ball in, but Carson and fellow linebacker Carl Banks held them out. It was one of the great defensive stands in Giants' history. The Broncos wound up coming away with no points. And the Giants won their first Super Bowl.

It will take those plays, ones that will live forever, to keep the Giants and me heading toward the Super Bowl. Plays like these, five of the team's greatest defensive exploits:

1. January 7, 2001. Giants 20, Eagles 10. NFC Division Playoff. Jason Sehorn makes a 32-yard, tumbling, tipped interception TD return.
2. January 4, 1987. Giants 49, 49ers 3. NFC Semifinal. Defensive Lineman Jim Burt knocks San Francisco QB Joe Montana unconscious.
3. December 21, 1958. Giants 10, Browns 0. Eastern Conference Playoff. Giants hold Jim Brown to eight yards on seven carries.
4. January 20, 1991. Giants 15, 49ers 13. NFC Championship. Erik Howard's hit causes San Francisco running back Roger Craig to fumble with just 2:36 to play, and L. T. recovers.
5. November 27, 1927. Giants 10, Bears 7. With the score tied 7–7 in the championship game, Chicago drives to the Giants' one-yard line, but Steve Owen and Cal Hubbard keep the Bears out of the end zone. Hinkey Haines then fakes a punt from his own end zone and completes a 58-yard pass to Charlie Corgan that sets up the Giants' winning score for the team's first championship.

Every team has one great game in it. And a great game would beat Philadelphia. The Giants don't even need great, actually. Just very good would do. And to be very good they simply need to play mistake-free football and hope that the Eagles don't.

Philadelphia, like Dallas, is finishing the year using a different QB than it started the season with. The Giants' nemesis, Donovan McNabb, went down with a knee injury and the team is in the hands of his backup, Jeff Garcia. Garcia's days as a bona fide starter are past. Ordinarily, McNabb's absence would be cause for optimism. But Garcia has played with élan for more than a month, catapulting the team, once 2–4, back into the playoffs. The Eagles have displayed the grit the Giants lack.

It is raining. The field is slippery, the ball slick. All the Giants need is one break. One tipped ball. One penalty that goes their way. One dropped pass. One fumble from Garcia or their pocket running back Brian Westbrook (the Eagles' version of Tiki). One interception.

The Giants receive the kickoff. The first snap is a false-start penalty on left tackle Dave Diehl. First-and-15.

Diehl wouldn't normally be taking Luke Pettigout's spot as Eli Manning's prime pass protector at left tackle. That assignment would normally go to Bob Whitfield, a bright, colorful, fifteen-year veteran and an overall No. 8 pick out of Stanford who owns a highly regarded recording studio in Atlanta. "You can either be good-looking in the face or good-looking in the wallet," he said, claiming to be happy with the latter as a sign of all he's accomplished. When Pettigout limped out of the locker room on crutches after the Chicago game, Whitfield stood at his stall and talked about his responsibilities coming off the bench. "For the team to be successful, the individual has to do his job," he said, "and all I have to do is go out there and make my blocks."

But in two games as a sub Whitfield was flagged for head-butting, rendering himself such an unstable liability he couldn't be put on a football field. It's quite possible he's the only sub ever to lead a team in head butts. It's not only inexcusable in a veteran, it makes you wonder whether Whitfield literally is trying to take himself off the field. Small though Whitfield's part is in the story of the season, his behavior is the most unpardonable of all.

Diehl's behavior by comparison is a small misstep. He is normally a guard and, playing left tackle in place of Whitfield, actually got tangled up in his own feet, tripped, and fell, untouched, on his first attempt at pass protection one week ago.

Manning follows the Diehl penalty with his first pass, a 29-yard completion to Burress, taking the Giants into Eagles' territory. A second pass, a flip to Tiki, takes them to the 34-yard line, but again, and so true to form, another penalty, a hold against center O'Hara, pushes them back. Three plays, two penalties.

Tiki runs right for 8 yards, runs left for 2 more and, following a quarterback sneak, the Giants have overcome O'Hara's penalty and got themselves a first down at the 32. Tiki runs right, finds a crease and takes it to the 17. And on the next play Manning finds Burress in the end zone for a touchdown.

The Giants jump out to a 7–0 lead!

Oh, no.

I'm not hounding anyone for gratitude here, but I've tried not to tangle up the reader with too many statistical impediments, the kind that tend to stretch like barbed wire through the pages of many books, rendering them impassable. But to illustrate how confounding the team's performance has been, you need to know this one stat: For the fourteenth time in seventeen games, the Giants have scored first.

The Giants usually score first and score easily and then lose. Some epitaph.

Watching the rest of the first quarter is like watching a locksmith grind a duplicate key. Each curve and bend and notch follows a template.

Philly goes three-and-out, punts, and the Giants begin their second possession on the Eagles' 49. A great chance to add to their lead and drain the opponent's confidence. But two more penalties and two incomplete passes and the Giants give the ball back.

Again the Eagles go three-and-out, punt and the Giants begin their third possession near the 50. Another chance to pad their lead. This time they don't even advance into field-goal range and have to kick.

Again the Eagles go three-and-out, punt and the Giants begin their fourth possession of the first quarter on the Philadelphia 46. Another chance to pad their lead. By now, with the first quarter not yet over, the Giants 7–0 lead could have been 21–0. Should be at least 14–0, given the field position they've enjoyed.

On first down from the 46, the Giants throw in their obligatory flat pass to fullback Jim Finn, an innocuous play they run once or so a game and that picks up maybe five yards, if it's completed. This one isn't. The sure touch Eli demonstrated on the first drive of the game has deserted him.

On second-and-10 Tiki is dropped for a three-yard loss. On third-and-13, Manning passes to Tim Carter way short of any hope for a first down, causing me to wonder what the hell Carter and Eli are thinking. The Giants are forced to punt from the Eagles' 49.

As Jeff Feagles' foot cracks into the ball, sending it back over to the Eagles, who run out the first quarter with it, a sick feeling floods my heart.

The sick feeling reminds me of a TV show I once worked on. It was a show about car salesmen. A group of guys who knew all the angles. In the pilot script the main character wagers he can sell a car to someone. And in the very first shot of the production, he descends a flight of stairs to the floor of the showroom with his eye on the prize—the resistant mark.

The director yelled, "Action," and I watched the actor descend the stairs, and I knew right then the show wasn't going to be a winner. The script was brilliant (I hadn't written it, rest assured) and the cast was beyond sensational. But I saw a look in the actor's eye as he walked down the stairs. It wasn't the look of a guy licking his chops. It was the look of a guy just walking down a flight of stairs, going through the motions. And I got this sick feeling watching the first shot, realizing we wouldn't hit paydirt.

If there is anything the Giants have not done this season it's lick their chops, display a killer instinct. A championship-caliber team would have begun the second quarter of this play-off game up by anywhere from 10 to 24 points, with its boot on Philadelphia's neck, a rout on and the stadium jail rapidly filling with angry drunks, Maced, pepper-sprayed, their skulls cracked by the cops' nightsticks, and puking up cheesesteak on their own shoes. But all the Giants seem capable of achieving is nourishing an opponent's hopes and confidence at the expense of their own. The Eagles know they have taken the Giants' best punch, and that for the next three quarters all they need to do is work the game and wait for the Giants to falter.

Sure enough, by the fourth quarter the Eagles are in command, 20–10, and the Giants are on the ropes. Now the rain is pounding and you can feel the clock winding down on the scoreboard ticking in your heart. With 12:13 to play, down by 7, Eli leads his offense out onto the field. The ball is on the Giants' 20.

Behind the press box, sitting in the media cafeteria, Archie Manning stares at a TV on the wall and watches his youngest boy break the huddle. Archie wants to be by himself for this. Whether you are Archie Manning or Sam Fusco, you are cognizant of the same hard truth: If Eli Manning has something to give this team, if there's anything going on upstairs, he'd better let it out now. He must answer the question.

Tiki Barber lines up for the last drive of his career. He has nothing to prove. He has been playing football pretty much since he can remember and this is the end of it. His brother Ronde is here watching the game and next year for the first time the twins' lives will split apart. They will not be doing the same thing.

Tiki runs hard, looking for the crease. He carries twice for eighteen yards, continuing to slam into defenders Jeremiah Trotter and Brian Dawkins until the end. He is a warrior. A defensive holding penalty gives the Giants a first down at their 46.

It is just grinding and rain now and the clock ticking down and men launching themselves at each other like pit bulls. I don't know how Archie can stand watching. I'm chewing the inside of my mouth to ribbons. At least Eli seems to have his rhythm back. Facing third-and-4, he completes a pass to Carter and the Giants have a first down at the Philadelphia 34.

Tiki carries left for three, catches a pass for six more. Facing another third down, Tiki churns into the left side of the line and gets another first down. Tiki has gotten the ball on six of the Giants' nine plays.

Eli and Tiki are coaxing the Giants down the field. But then, on three straight plays, the Giants' offensive linemen are penalized. False starts on Diehl and on Chris Snee and, to top it all, a short pass that Tiki takes all the way to the Philly 14 is called back by another flag against Snee, this time for holding.

Three straight penalties. On the most important drive of the season.

It is first-and-30. After an incompletion, it's second-and-30. Which is reminiscent of the pivotal third-and-22 the Giants allowed the Bears to convert and that seemed to start the Giants on a downward spiral that has dumped them out unceremoniously here: on the Eagles' 43, with just over six minutes left in the season, facing an almost insurmountable situation.

Tiki's runs have to be shelved now. It's going to depend on Eli's passing. On the kid's arm. And on the only bullet left in the gun: Plaxico Burress.

The Eagles are salivating, like they do in one of those chunky soup commercials that McNabb's mom stars in. They storm after Eli at the snap, but he steps left and finds Burress to get back eighteen of those thirty yards. Burress is playing an extraordinary game. And still facing a daunting third-and-12, Eli rockets Burress another pass in the left flat. Burress puts a great move on his defender and is pushed out of bounds after a 14-yard gain at the 11. There are five and a half minutes left.

Improbably, Eli and Burress have overcome a second-and-30. It is the team's third third-down conversion on the drive. My throat is scratchy and dry. My pulse is pounding.

Playing a hot hand, Burress is called on yet again. And from the Philadelphia press box at the opposite end of the stadium, as Eli fades back to pass on this gut-check drive, I watch it unfold perfectly:

Burress streaks down the left hash mark. His defender is playing off Burress's right shoulder and no help is visible underneath toward the corner. Eli immediately reads this passing lane to Burress's left, outside shoulder and steps up into the pocket. He rifles a pass to Burress streaking into the end zone.

Touchdown!

The Giants have tied the score with 5:08 left to play. They have fought back.

Almost half a year ago, on an early-summer morning at the tail end of July back in Albany, Eli uncorked his first pass of the season, a perfect, spiraling rainbow that was completed. Now, at 7:42 P.M. on a cold, rainy night in Philadelphia on January 7, he has thrown his last pass of the season.

It, too, is complete. And, best of all, it is a touchdown. Capping a 13-play, 80-yard drive, facing a do-or-die situation.

Unfortunately, it comes fives minutes too soon. The Eagles have five minutes to untie the score against a Giants' defense that has all too often not been able to stop its opponents.

Play after play Eagles QB Garcia eludes the rush. Play after play Westbrook carries the ball down the field toward winning field-goal position.

Someone make a play.

Someone stop this from happening.
Don't let us lose.

I am in my den back home on Long Island, my ear cocked to that same bulky, brown Bakelite radio beside which I'd first fallen in love with this team alongside my father and brother. This time I am listening to the 1958 championship game, ready for my innocent life to continue on its untarnished way. Except that some malign force with which I have no prior experience, embodied in a guy named Johnny Unitas, some guy named Raymond Berry, some team from a nowheresville called Baltimore can't be contained by my heroes Andy Robustelli and Sam Huff and Cliff Livingston and Jim Katcavage.

I cannot look up and meet my father's eyes. I want to spare him the painful sight of my devastation, which is compounded by the knowledge that he is, as the clock counts down, helpless to fix it. If I look at my dad I might cry because I don't feel tough enough not to, and I should be, goddammit, I'm nine.

I sneak a glance at my brother. He looks pained, but not ready to cry like I am. He and my father are talking normally, but my throat is choked with phlegm. My brother and father are both Giants fans. They should feel the way I do. Why don't they feel as bad? Aren't they ready to cry, too? Aren't their tears beading on their lashes? I can't look at them.

We're going to lose. I can hardly breathe.

I gaze around the press box trying to resituate myself in the present world, among grown-ups tapping away at their laptops, exchanging the dark jokes reporters do, as the Eagles line up to try a field goal that can win the game. I am surprised to find myself wet-eyed.

There is the usual stampede to the locker room like the running of the bulls at Pamplona. The others are running because they are on deadline. I am running because I have waited all year for this, Tiki's last moment. I need to observe Tiki closely so I can learn how to deal when there are no more creases to run through.

I try to keep up through the tunnels hampered by my bum hips when some reporter tugs at me and yells, "You dropped something," and points behind us.

My underpants. I'd hurriedly stuffed all the stat sheets and notebooks back into my shoulder bag before joining my fellow stampeders. I'd left the bag open and now the entire thundering herd of the Fourth Estate has rumbled over my briefs and kicked them aside. I retrieve them. There are sportswriters' footprints all over them. I dispose of the trampled briefs and rejoin the throng in the visitors' locker, where the Giants are showering and packing. With quiet, glum faces they are accepting the fact that David Akers's field goal sailed straight through the uprights and ended the season for Big Blue. Philadelphia 23, Giants 20.

The Eagles' owner, Jeff Lurie, enters and seeks out Tiki to offer congratulatory final words. Tiki dons a suit, not looking pained to have taken off his Giants jersey for the final time. He is at peace. In a black trench coat, GM Ernie Accorsi makes his way through the knots of reporters and players. Accorsi stands for a moment in the middle of the room. He is a man with a large head and an overturned bowl of dark black hair, and his neck seems to swivel around now, birdlike, taking in the blur of dressing players and the steam from the showers. He went all out this season, played every card and farthing he had for this, his last game, after more than four decades in various front offices. But no sooner had the Eagles kicked the winning field goal on the very last play of the game than all the players in this locker room became Ernie Accorsi's no longer. Their contracts, their injuries, their divorces, their dustups, their futures, and that of their team are no longer his professional concern.

"The defense sure didn't act like Eli's last touchdown drive was anything special" is the most grumbling Eli's proud dad Archie will allow later about the way the season ended.

The season is a wrap. Everyone looks numb and bewildered, the way you are in the first few moments after coming to a sudden stop. But this was not a shattering loss. Over the last five months they've become too acquainted with mistakes and losing to be stunned. And soon there is the understandable relief any actor or crew member or anyone feels at the end of an all-consuming, grueling season that is at last over. Next stop: the beach.

Accorsi shakes hands with players, congratulates Tiki on his great career, stuffs his hands deep into his black coat pockets and leaves the National Football League after thirty-seven years.

Suddenly, oddly, I feel like the only person in this mad scene who has no idea what to do next. I feel utterly aimless. At a loss. I find myself standing beside Ronde Barber. From now on, one way to tell the twins apart is that Ronde is the brother with the Super Bowl ring.

As if reading my desolation, Ronde tries cheering me up. "It's hard to be too emotional about this being his last game," he says. "Tiki knew the stakes. We all knew the stakes. We all knew it was going to end, but you have to look at it as a new beginning. A new phase of life."

Tiki "goes to the podium" for the last time as a Giant, on the heels of an encomium from Shockey, who says, "Tiki's one of the greatest players I've ever played with and it's just an honor to be around him. He's not the fastest guy or the strongest guy or the biggest guy, but he's got twice the size heart of anyone in this league."

Shockey exits, and it's impossible to imagine him heading toward anything other than the ether. Is there really an off-season for Jeremy Shockey? Or does he simply disappear into the rain forest or into some cave atop Mount Olympus or some titanium tube where he waits in suspended animation until next year?

Shockey!

"Maybe sadness will hit me at private moments when I can sit and recollect and enjoy what I've done for ten years," Tiki tells the reporters. He looks not just completely at peace with his decision, but happy. "For the longest time I thought my career was meaningless unless I had that Super Bowl ring. I didn't get a Super Bowl ring. And for a long time I thought that was going to define me. And I've come to the conclusion that it's not going to define me. My legacy is going to be that despite the ups and the downs, the good times and the bad, I've never walked out on that field without leaving it all on the field. And that's what most of the players I've played against and the fans who watch me, that's what they see."

Returning across the hall to the locker room, Tiki picks up his gear and heads for the exit. But before he leaves he is steered into a small, adjacent storage room. There have been innumerable celebrations and huzzahs, not to mention brickbats, sent Tiki's way in the weeks leading up to this moment, but nothing seems as appropriate as the one last gesture a locker room attendant offers Tiki.

There is a low beam running across the length of the ceiling. Squinting up, Tiki sees dozens of names scrawled. The men who have come before him, who have played and won or lost here, have left one simple reminder of the life in football they lived.

The beam is covered with their signatures. Curtis Martin, the running back of the Pats and Jets. The linebacker Willie McGinest. A few coaches: Tennessee's Jeff Fisher and the Cowboys' Jimmy Johnson. Along with some older players, like Billy "White Shoes" Johnson. And, also, some who have made the plays that live forever.

I explain to Ronde who Tommy Nobis is, the first linebacker ever chosen No. 1 in the NFL draft and the first pick of the new Atlanta Falcons franchise in 1966 before the Barber brothers were born. And there's the signature of the immortal quarterback Sonny Jurgensen. They have all hurt and healed and, ultimately, removed their pads and passed them on to others and left their names on this beam to say they, too, came this way and left it all on the field.

Tiki is handed a pen. And a chair to stand on so he can reach high enough. As Ronde and I watch, the greatest Giant running back of all stretches on his tiptoes and signs out: Tiki Barber 21.

It is a long, dark walk through the rain to the Broad Street subway blocks from the Linc. My own last, sodden stumble over empty beer bottles.

Philadelphia losses are the worst. It all goes back to 1960 and Bednarik. When the Giants lose to the Eagles I feel like Bednarik just hit me. I'm lifeless. Splayed out on the field. Maybe dead.

The year Frank Gifford had to take off after that, the Giants were still good enough to make it to the NFL championship game. In the kitchenette of a motel room in Miami Beach on New Year's Eve, 1961, I watched the Giants get killed 37–0 by the Packers. I could stay up until midnight and wear a hat, but I didn't have the heart.

I remind myself of that misery, slouching toward Broad Street in the rain. How I'd watched that game under silent, bitter protest—if only Gifford had been able to play. That seems suddenly stupid. They lost 37–0. How would anything have made a difference?

That's what I'm thinking as I reach the station. I realize I don't have exact change, but an attendant takes one look at me haplessly patting my pockets and the water dripping off my head and trickling from my pants cuffs, and she smiles and waves me through for free.

"Senior discount," she says, in a holiday spirit.

I sit on the train, smiling to myself. Somehow, between the Linc and the subway, I've changed. The cashier up on the sidewalk mistook me for a fifty-seven-year-old man instead of a boy.

Each man is the sportswriter of his own life, writing down the plays that will live forever. Well, we're at the last stop for the Giants. And the last for me.

I ride the Broad Street line north to meet a friend. The car is full of celebrating Philadelphia fans thundering: "Giants suck! Giants suck!" It is deafening. I cannot think of a worse place to be.

On the Broad Street line in Philadelphia, I am truly mindful of the certainty of my own death. That's the legal lingo they use in wills, as my probate attorney Newmark has taught me. He's the guy who sent me out on my trek. On this self-audit of my history with the Giants. But I will survive this ride. And so, I think, it's come time to answer the question I posed to myself starting out in Albany.

Who was that boy?

He was fiercely sweet. He loved his team so hard he thought he'd break. But he didn't break. Just say this: He got me this far.

The train lurches forward and the subway wheels screech hellishly. My cell phone rings. It's my daughter.

"Are you okay, Dad?" is the first thing she wants to know.

"Never been better, kiddo," I say.

Acknowledgments

Madness of this sort can never be wrought by one man alone. I'm deeply grateful to the always-professional Giants staff, especially Pat Hanlon, Peter John-Baptiste, and Avis Roper. And to Harry Carson and Frank Gifford, John Johnson, Ernie Accorsi, Allie Sherman, and Chris Mara among many in the Giants' extended family who took the time to speak with me. Tiki Barber was a model of grace under pressure and a friend of this endeavor.

There are many good books about football in its different eras. I was stoked by many sources. Foremost, Fred Exley's *A Fan's Notes*. Richard Whittingham's *Illustrated History of the Giants*. Carlo DeVito's *Wellington: The Maras, the Giants, and the City of New York*; *Manning: Archie and Peyton Manning*, with John Underwood; *LT: Over the Edge*, with Steve Serby. Phil Simms's *Sunday Morning Quarterback*, with Vic Carucci. And I'm grateful for the light shed by so many other books, including James T. Farrell's *Studs Lonigan*; Roger Kahn's extraordinary Dempsey bio, *A Flame of Pure Fire*; and Jack Cavanaugh's splendid *Tunney*.

Through the help of the *New York Times*'s Pulitzer Prize–winning sports columnist Dave Anderson, Mr. Cavanaugh was kind enough to talk with me about Tim Mara's onetime partner, Billy Gibson, the colorful fight manager. I should say here that in no place I'm aware of is there a detailed account of the meeting where Mara was first offered a New York franchise in the National Football League. It took place against the backdrop of sharp-elbowed, political maneuvering to promote the first Dempsey-Tunney fight. And Mara's shrewd musing about how little $500 seemed for a franchise that covered a city so immense is the only line ever ascribed to any of the participants. The rest is reconstruction and surmise.

Bob Daley told me how Mara pronounced Tooney. He knows. He worked in the team's p.r. office. His dad, Arthur, a Pulitzer Prize–winning sports columnist for the *New York Times*, was a close friend of the Maras and was the team's public address announcer on December 7, 1941, at the Polo Grounds, where his summonses of military personnel who might be in the stands were the first clue to my father and mother in attendance that World War II had begun at Pearl Harbor. Bob Daley's 1967 novel *Only a Game* remains one of the best football novels. And I thank him for his generosity.

A slew of miscreants, professional and otherwise, aided and abetted me. The idea, perhaps conspiracy would be a better word, was hatched by my normally astute editor, David Hirshey. Beyond that, this book couldn't have happened if the following people had used good sense and refused to talk with me about it, boost my spirits, and done their utmost to see this never saw the light of day: Mark Reiter, of the PFD Group; Mark Lepselter; Michael Rizzo at ICM; Fred Schruers; Brock Walsh; Joy Horowitz; Susan Squire; Rob Fleder; Marilyn Johnson; Jay Lovinger; Bob Ward; David Schoenfield and Kevin Jackson at espn.com; George Blooston; Joey Goldstein; Hilary Lipsitz; Mary Choteborsky; Jarrod Taylor; Michael Solomon; Alan Richman; Zandes Hollander, Rachel Elinsky; John Wells; Joel Surnow; Vic Levin and Paul Reiser; Dale Hoffer; my friends at P. J. Clarke's; Professor Aryeh Kosman; Dr. Jane Fischer; Fordham's athletic director, Frank McLaughlin; Jeff Rothberg; Janne Sheridan Keyes; my mother, Phyllis; my sister, Lisa; and my nephew, Geoffrey Director.

Knowing this was in the hands of the ultimate Giants fan, HarperCollins sales dynamo Andrea Rosen, allowed me to sleep easy at night (between bouts of restless leg syndrome). I was also blessed by the invaluable assistance of my dear friend Gil Schwartz and by LeslieAnne Wade of CBS Sports. Every time it seemed I might be stopped short of the goal line, the indefatigable Kate Hamill dusted me off, dumped a bucket of water on my head, and dragged me into the end zone.

Above and beyond everything, here's to my two Super Bowl rings—my wife, Jan, who read many drafts and does not know how to be less than loving and honest; and my precious daughter, Chloe Pauline.